BBC MUSIC GUIDES

Tchaikovsky Symphonies and Concertos

JOHN WARRACK

BRITISH BROADCASTING CORPORATION

Published by the British Broadcasting Corporation
35 Marylebone High Street, London W1M 4AA

ISBN: 0 563 12773 2
First published 1969
Revised edition 1974
© John Warrack 1969 and 1974

In this second edition a new section
on *Manfred* has been added, the text has
been revised, and new translations of the
quotations have been made. All dates are
given in New Style.

Printed in England by
Cox & Wyman Ltd, London, Reading and Fakenham

BBC MUSIC GUIDES

———

TCHAIKOVSKY SYMPHONIES AND CONCERTOS

BBC MUSIC GUIDES

General Editor: LIONEL SALTER

TCHAIKOVSKY'S SYMPHONIC STYLE

In 1895 Hans Richter conducted the first performance in Vienna of Tchaikovsky's *Symphonie Pathétique,* and the occasion was duly reviewed by Eduard Hanslick. Despite Wagner's bitter caricature in *Die Meistersinger,* Hanslick was no Beckmesser but a critic who wrote out of a profound and open-minded loyalty to the German symphonic ideal. Although this was strong enough for him to be disturbed by the unusual order of the movements and even to complain that the 'disagreeable rhythm' of the 5/4 movement would be better if altered to 6/4, he was quick to sense the nature of the work's originality:

Although the usual sequence of the four movements of the symphony has its psychological reasons and is historically acknowledged, it is no iron barrier excluding exceptions or changes for all time. The criterion will always be whether or not the chosen order lacks psychological motivation or inner relationship. There is obviously a hidden poetical programme at the bottom of this symphony; the first movement, with its rhapsodic shifting between *adagio* and *allegro,* between major and minor, points to a passionate tragedy of the heart. Most listeners would probably wish for a programme to save them guessing; I consider it, rather, proof of the composer's musical temperament that he lets his music speak for itself and prefers to leave us guessing rather than force a laid-out course upon himself and us.

Tchaikovsky would have been grateful. He despised programme music, to the extent of reproaching himself for *The Tempest, Francesca da Rimini* and even *Romeo and Juliet*; yet he also declared that he did not want his symphonies to be an empty series of chords, rhythms and modulations, 'expressing' nothing. Music was never for him essentially a structural art, reflecting in the nature of its order something beyond the composer; and no more than any of his fellow-Romantics did he find the symphony his own instinctive form of expression. Though Schubert, Mendelssohn and (with the most difficulty) Brahms found it possible to reconcile their cast of mind to sonata form, symphony (in which the real test is grasp of sonata) is not the typical Romantic medium. The balance and architectural tension of sonata lay outside the Romantics' natural way of thinking, representing as they did a move away from the ordered society of the world before the French Revolution and the Enlightenment's belief that everything could be solved by reason, towards a more personal and more sensational art in which the highest value was now set upon feeling. An immediate consequence was loss of faith in sonata, and, for all the use to which it has successfully been put even in our own times, it was never again to be the natural means of expression for all composers. One of the qualities of Beethoven's greatness is his mastery in extending sonata to cover a wider tonal range that at the same time enlarged the form's dramatic and humanly expressive possibilities. But although it was recognition of this that led E. T. A. Hoffmann to claim Beethoven as a great Romantic, he represents a magnificent act of the will imposed upon a changing situation. For Wagner the Ninth Symphony was the superb climax of instrumental music, crying out for redemption by poetry; and he saw his music dramas as the symphony's natural heir. Many of Beethoven's contemporaries admired and resisted him in equal proportions, believing, like Weber, that his genius was occupying an area different from that which music should now explore. The characteristic Romantic structures are looser, more dramatic, reflecting visual and narrative elements, personal sensations and experiences. Hence opera is the central Romantic form; in instrumental music, whether with symphonic poem, the short atmospheric piano piece or a concerto in the shape of a free fantasy, the tendency was for music to evolve dramatically around some more or less precise programme or emotion.

But though Tchaikovsky was suspicious of programme music, he recognised the virtues of the symphony. Beethoven's Fifth Symphony was the conscious model of his own Fourth; Mozart was to him 'the Christ of Music'. In part this was the paradoxical Romantic longing for the lost order and balance of the classical world – Berlioz delighting in Gluck, Richard Strauss fancying himself kin to Mozart. To his patroness Nadezhda von Meck, who was shocked by his adoration of 'this sunny genius, whose music in remembrance moves me to tears', Tchaikovsky explained with candid self-perception:

You say that my worship of him is contrary to my musical nature, but perhaps it is just because as a child of my time I am broken, morally sick, that I search Mozart's music, which for the most part reveals that exceptional joy in life which was part of a nature sound, unified and *not disrupted by introspection*, for calm and consolation. On the whole it seems to me that in an artist's soul his creative ability is completely independent of his sympathy with this or that master. It is possible to love Beethoven, for instance, and by nature be closer to Mendelssohn. Could there be a more glaring instance of inconsistency, for instance, than Berlioz the composer and champion of ultra-Romanticism in music, and Berlioz the critic and adorer of Gluck? ... Do you know that Chopin did not care for Beethoven, and could hardly bear some of his works? I was told this by a man who knew him personally. At any rate, dissimilarity of temperament between two artists is no hindrance to their mutual sympathy.

But Tchaikovsky's attraction to the symphony also sprang from the clear perception that here was a form which could be modified to act, not as framework of a sort nor yet as an abstract construction, but as vehicle of his emotions. About the Fourth Symphony he wrote to Nadezhda von Meck:

There are certain kinds of composition which imply the use of familiar forms, for example *symphony*. Here I keep in general outline to the usual traditional forms, but only in general outline, i.e. the sequence of the work's movements. The details can be treated very freely, if this is demanded by the development of the ideas.

He also recognises this symphony to be in a sense programmatic, in that it embodies experience rather than acting as a pure exercise of the musical imagination; and when Taneyev objected that it 'gives the effect of a symphonic poem to which the composer has slapped on three more movements', he amplified his observation that he disliked the notion of symphonies as mere progressions of musical devices:

Most assuredly my symphony has a programme, but one that cannot be expressed in words: the very attempt would be ludicrous. But is this not proper to a symphony, the most purely lyrical of musical forms? Should not a symphony reveal those wordless urges that hide in the heart, asking earnestly for expression?

When Nadezhda von Meck, who was privately well aware of his homosexuality, asked him if he had 'known non-Platonic love', he replied:

Yes and no. If this question were put slightly differently, i.e. asking if I have known complete happiness in love, the answer would be: *No, no and no ! ! !* However, I think that it is in my music that the answer to your question lies. If you asked me if I have understood the whole power, the whole immeasurable strength of this feeling, the answers would be: *Yes, yes and yes*, reiterating that I have passionately tried more than once to express in music the agony and at the same time ecstasy of love. Whether I have succeeded in this, I do not

7

know, or, rather, I leave to others to judge. I completely disagree with you that music *cannot fully communicate one's feelings of love*. I hold the complete contrary, that *only music alone can* achieve this. You say that *words* are necessary. Oh no! Words alone are not enough, and where they are powerless there appears fully armed a more eloquent language, i.e. music. That verse form to which poets resort to express love is a usurpation of that territory belonging wholly to music. *Words* confined to the form of poetry cease to be simply *words*: they become music ... Your observation that words often merely harm music, dragging it down from unscaleable heights, is absolutely true. I have always felt it deeply, and that is perhaps why I have succeeded better with instrumental works than with vocal.

So for Tchaikovsky 'the most lyrical of musical forms' meant the one in which his feelings could most completely be framed, expressing longings and ideas which were too vague for words and needed the eloquence of music. Fundamentally, his conception of music was the lyrical idea, namely melody, complete even to its harmonic and orchestral clothing, as he told Nadezhda von Meck shortly after the Fourth Symphony:

A melody can never appear except with its attendant harmony. On the whole both these elements of music, together with the rhythm, are never separate from one another, i.e. every melodic idea brings with it its implied harmony and certainly its rhythmic structure ... As to instrumentation, if it is for orchestra, the musical idea appears already coloured by a certain scoring.

Writing again on the following day he confesses that having found the idea he must often then alter it so that it fits the requirements of the form, even if this means destroying things written with love and inspiration; he acknowledges his lack of skill with form, and that he was at the time careless with his material. He recognises, too, that '*exemplary forms* my works will never be; I can only improve, not fully eradicate the essential characteristics of my musical make-up.'

But Tchaikovsky's trouble with form goes deeper than the conception of ideas that may not be amenable to sonata form. It arises from his being too successful a melodist. Beethoven could construct a complete movement out of something anyone could have thought of, such as the opening themes of the *Eroica* and Fifth Symphonies; though only he saw their far-reaching possibilities over the span of a large-scale sonata movement, and only he had the patience and creative toughness to work them. Tchaikovsky's basic act of invention was not structural and hence symphonic, but melodic. The melody that is of itself complete will obviously not be susceptible of development: as Taneyev pointed out, it can do little more than be repeated; though it can be repeated and modified with sufficient ingenuity in the hands of a master such as Tchaikovsky to create interest, tension and satisfaction over a large span. The problem is more acute still when folk-song is used, or at least lies behind the invention as in the early symphonies. Unlike a genuine nationalist such as Mussorgsky who saw folk-song as part of the collective national subconscious, Tchaikovsky liked folk-songs simply because they reminded him of his mother, who had died when he was 14, and his sister – 'those angels come down from Heaven' – and the security of his country childhood. To Nadezhda von Meck he explained:

On the whole, as far as the Russian element in my music is concerned, i.e. the relationship between the national songs and my melodies and harmonies, this is because I grew up in the backwoods, from earliest childhood saturated with the indescribable beauty of the characteristic traits of Russian folk music . . .

He tends to regard folk-song as something to be quoted or invoked, rather than used as a generative force. The extra problem it brings into his style lies with the inclination of Russian folk-song to repeat itself, using similar intervals and phrases with an almost ritual insistence, creating a static effect rather than one geared to movement and purpose. The melody tends, in fact, to become something near a set of variations on itself, to proceed by modification rather than development or contrast; and this clearly makes it recalcitrant to symphonic development. The obsessive thirds of Russian folk-song permeate Tchaikovsky's tunes; and clearly he was also haunted by the plagal tendencies of Russian folk-song, so strongly does the interval of the falling fourth colour his invention in the early symphonies, always prominently placed in the melodies and acting as emotional coloration rather than implying a harmonic progression. A single example from each of the first three symphonies will show the characteristic, the second being an actual folk-tune:

9

EX. I

In the last of these it is clear that behind the *Ländler* idea lies a Tchaikovsky waltz; but behind the waltz in turn lies the flavour of Russian folk-song. There is an obvious difference between the feeling common to each of these tunes and the march in the *Pathétique,* which though constructed almost entirely out of fourths is fully emancipated from the peasant background.

EX. 4

Belief in melody as the most lyrical and therefore fundamental musical idea further imposes a limitation on Tchaikovsky's harmony. It is not that he is clumsy or lacking in resource when it comes to conceiving the harmony along with the tune, though he is prone to short sequences of chords, usually moving between the tonic and the dominant, or even to a plain alternation of two chords, as at the start of the First Piano Concerto. But this habit tends to show not merely in accompanying tunes but in the structure of complete movements: the fundamental harmony of the opening movement of the Fifth Symphony is a perpetual swing between tonic and subdominant – the 'fourths' feeling translated into structural terms. Tchaikovsky, in fact, does not sense the large-scale pulls and the subtler smaller tensions of the tonal system over a complete movement, as is the German characteristic. At least he was self-aware enough, this most bitterly self-aware of composers, to realise it, and late in his career he was still bewailing his difficulties:

All my life I have been much troubled by my inability to grasp and manipulate form in music. I fought hard against this defect and can say with pride that I have achieved some progress, but I shall end my days without having ever written anything that is perfect in form. What I write has always a mountain of padding: an experienced eye can detect the thread in the seams and I can do nothing about it.

Because of these defects which he recognised only too acutely, Tchaikovsky was obliged to make his own compromise with sonata form as well as with the traditional layout of the symphony. In each of the symphonies except the First he chooses to begin with a slow, atmospheric introduction that immediately lays a claim on the mood of the listener rather than alerting him to a piece of musical action. In the Second Symphony it is the unaccompanied horn tune of Ex. 2; in the Third a funeral march; the Fourth and Fifth open with the 'fate' themes that come to pervade them, the Sixth on a sombre *adagio*. The sonata movement which ensues tends to fall into a similar pattern from symphony to symphony: there is a first subject which, since it cannot readily be developed, is subjected to repetitions in which new orchestration and changes in emotional emphasis do duty for development, then comes a long transition; then the second subject, in more lyrical vein, is similarly extended; a second long transition follows; finally both themes are recapitulated and the movement is rounded off with a coda. This, it can be seen, is really an ingenious episodic treatment of two tunes rather than a symphonic development of them. They do not act upon each other, and because of this and because of their self-sufficient nature they impose a comparatively mechanical role upon the passages where the substance of a symphonic movement properly resides. Instead of being involved in an organic, evolutionary process, Tchaikovsky is driven to use devices more or less only for the sake of generating expectation of the next entry of a tune – ostinato figures, dramatic pedal-points, sequences that screw anticipation up to fever pitch with each new step, all expressed in frenzied rhythmic activity. The tune thus re-introduced must obviously live up to expectation by being even more sensationally scored, and perhaps given new intensity by a passionately throbbing accompaniment figure or anguished fluctuations of tempo from bar to bar coupled with urgent expressive instructions, so that it comes to seem on the verge of words or, at any rate, tears. A classic instance comes in the *andante cantabile* of the Fifth Symphony, where the secondary theme returns with almost frantic emotional markings occurring every two bars.

EX. 5

Despite the *fff* and the *con tutta forza* markings, the straining upward progression at the end of this example leads three bars later to another return of the theme now marked *ffff*. It is a clear instance of 'a symphony revealing those wordless urges that hide in the heart, asking earnestly for expression'.

The motivic 'fate' themes of the Fourth and Fifth Symphonies notwithstanding, there is no relationship between Tchaikovsky's symphonic movements. The central pair of movements (only the Third has five movements) tends to assume the ballet style that was never far from his mind and indeed proved the source of some of his most beautiful inspirations. There is the pizzicato movement of the Fourth Symphony, possibly inspired by Delibes's *Sylvia* as much as by the sound of the balalaika, the waltz in the Fifth and the near-waltz of the Sixth Symphony's 5/4 movement. The world of the ballet was consciously his escape from reality, as he acknowledged to Nadezhda von Meck in connection with the second subject of the Fourth Symphony's opening movement, itself candidly marked *in movimento di valse:*

> Would it not be better to turn away from reality and plunge into dreams? O, joy! at last a sweet and tender vision appears. Some bright, gracious human form passes and beckons somewhere.

Yet he saw this as part of the same symphonic experience, and found no difference between the idiom of symphony and that of ballet or opera or programme music; indeed, the march in the Second Symphony originated in the opera *Undine,* while the *alla tedesca* of the Third was to reappear in *Hamlet.* Tchaikovsky was justly proud of his ballet music, believing that the symphonies were not fundamentally different in kind but tackled a personal, real drama that was decorative and illusory in the ballets; and his operatic ideal was far removed from the Wagnerian symphonic fusion of poetry and music – he thought *Götterdämmerung* inferior to Delibes, reproaching Wagner for his lack of long melody. Already in the 1860s he had been much excited by the operatic fare of St Petersburg, which consisted principally of Verdi, Rossini and Meyerbeer; 1876 found him in Paris, revelling with what his brother Modest was to call 'an almost unhealthy passion' in *Carmen.* Possibly French blood inherited from his grandmother, certainly his intrinsic love of lucidity, brilliance and elegance coupled to a sense of fateful erotic tension, drew him to a work in which he found not the dispassionate searching for new effects that troubled him in his Russian contemporaries, but novelty genuinely linked to intense feeling:

> It is charming and delightful from beginning to end. Piquant harmonies, completely new combinations of many sounds, but this isn't their exclusive purpose. Bizet is an artist who pays tribute to modernity, but he is fired with true inspiration. And what a marvellous subject for an opera! I can't play the final scene without tears. On the one hand, the crowd enjoying itself and coarsely making merry as they watch the bullfight, on the other, a terrible tragedy and the death of the two principals who, through fate, *fatum,* ultimately reach the peak of their suffering and their inescapable end.

It is not hard to see the composer of the last three symphonies in this comment, nor surprising to find in them the influence of Verdi, of Meyerbeer in some of the piquant violence of the scoring, of Delibes and Massenet in some of his *larmoyant* phrases, but above all of Bizet. Elements of *Carmen* pervade the later symphonies, colouring the dramatic atmosphere and cropping up as direct influences – perhaps most strikingly in the second subject of the Sixth Symphony's opening movement, which in its general outline and its reliance upon a throbbing accompaniment to a gracefully curving melody is kin to the world of the Flower Song. The Fourth Symphony came the year after he heard *Carmen,* and there can be little doubt that the opera gave him henceforth in his symphonies an example of how a sense of fate and of emotional despair might be expressed in music that would not in the process forfeit elegance and even charm.

THE FIRST THREE SYMPHONIES

Symphony No. 1 in G minor

Tchaikovsky was right to congratulate himself, however wryly, on having made progress in the handling of symphonic form throughout his career. All the same, he retained a warm affection for his First Symphony, feeling it to be immature but in some ways richer than many of his later works. It was born out of much travail. Possibly encouraged by the success of Tchaikovsky's overture for full orchestra in 1866, a rearrangement of a student overture, Rubinstein urged him to write a symphony and managed to fire him with such enthusiasm for the idea that sketches were begun in the same month. The mood of optimism was abruptly shattered by César Cui's withering review of the cantata that had been Tchaikovsky's graduation piece. Cast into gloom, he forced himself to continue work, spending all his days and his sleepless nights at the task until the inevitable breakdown ensued: a doctor called in to treat him found him 'on the verge of madness' and considered the case hopeless. But despite hallucinations, an overpowering sense of dread and physical symptoms such as numbness in his hands and feet, he continued writing and by the summer was able to show the all-but-completed work to his former teachers Anton Rubinstein and Nicholas Zaremba. Though bitterly disappointed by their comments, he seems not to have been so cast down as by the previous setback, and set about revising it in accordance with their recommendations. In November they declared the second and third movements to be fit for performance; the scherzo met with a poor reception in December, but the two movements were warmly applauded in St Petersburg in February. The complete work did not receive a performance until the following 15 February in Moscow, under Nikolay Rubinstein. Though naturally pleased with this painfully achieved success, Tchaikovsky further revised and cut the work in 1874; this final version was performed in Moscow under Max Erdmannsdörfer on 1 December 1883.

In 1862 Mendelssohn's piano works were published in Moscow by Jürgenson as part of the first standard edition of the German classics in Russia. Tchaikovsky must have studied them: his distaste for Brahms and Wagner did not extend to Mendelssohn, whose example stands behind much in this symphony. Not only is there a Mendelssohnian grace of invention, but the influence shows both in the lightness and pace of the scherzo (an orchestral version of a movement from a C sharp minor Piano Sonata), particularly in the neatly managed close (which is straight from the world of *A Midsummer Night's Dream*), and in the elegantly flowing melody of the very opening with its nimble answer over rustling strings. Furthermore, if Tchaikovsky knew Mendelssohn's *Italian* and *Scottish* Symphonies, he must have been impressed by their skill in transmuting into symphonic form a personal experience arising out of emotion at a romantic landscape. His own symphony is entitled 'Winter Daydreams', with subtitles to each of the first two movements, 'Dreams of a winter journey' and 'Land of desolation, land of mists'. The country explored is, of course, his own Russia; and though the last two movements have little to suggest that the idea was carried through very thoroughly, the atmosphere of the symphony is closer to Mendelssohn than to anything else in the symphonic tradition.

It is, nevertheless, wholly characteristic of Tchaikovsky, not only in the appearance as trio to the scherzo of a typical and charming waltz, but in many of the fingerprints of his mature style. Together with a certain stiffness in handling sonata form and a fugato in the finale that is decently worked rather than organic and structural, there are already present habits which were to mark his more ambitious works. The oboe tune of the *adagio* is accompanied by little flute scales of a kind that were to decorate many of his themes; and there is the familiar tendency to allow skilful orchestration to do the work of development for a tune that is complete in its own right. If this movement plays something of the same role as the 'Pilgrims' march' of the *Italian Symphony* or the 'Holyrood' *adagio* of the *Scottish Symphony,* there is more reliance on the strength of the melody alone to carry the expressive weight. Throughout, the accompaniments show an inclination, which Tchaikovsky was later to develop for more intense emotional purposes, to move between the principal chords of the key by step – the descending chromatic bass built into the answer to the opening theme, the scale figures that run under the second part of the scherzo theme, the harmonisation of the tune when the finale reaches its first *allegro* in rising scales, most originally the return of the *andante*

16

lugubre from the opening of this movement when the theme (with its characteristic falling fourth) is joined to the renewed *allegro* by a long passage whose suspense is brilliantly and economically created entirely by scales in conjunct motion over horn pedals. Whatever its shortcomings, the work has a freshness and charm unique among the symphonies. Tchaikovsky was right to remember it with affection: he came to achieve greater triumphs and to solve his symphonic problems more convincingly, but he did not again capture its peculiar innocence and simplicity. 'I have a soft spot for it,' he told a friend in 1883, 'for it is a sin of my sweet youth.'

Symphony No. 2 in C minor

Although Tchaikovsky cannot be accounted a nationalist composer in the sense that Mussorgsky and the rest of the 'Mighty Handful' were, he retained his love of Russian folk-song and of the chants of the Orthodox Church all his life. His religious music includes a setting of the Liturgy of St John Chrysostom and a Vesper Service that draws upon traditional chant; and his affection for folk-song led him in 1868–9 to publish in versions for piano duet *Fifty Russian Folksongs,* taken with one exception (which he transcribed himself) from the collections of Villebois and Balakirev. In 1872, making one of his regular visits to his sister Alexandra Davidov at Kamenka in the Ukraine, he began work on a Second Symphony; and the local songs he used in it led the critic Nikolay Kashkin to dub the work, after the contemporary nickname for the Ukraine, the 'Little Russian'.

However, Tchaikovsky's main concern in the symphony was neither to draw closer to the principles of the *Kuchka* nor to extend the mood of his First Symphony into a more particularised sense of Russia, but to improve his symphonic style. He had used folk-song from his early St Petersburg days and the Ostrovsky overture *The Storm*; he now saw it as valid symphonic material. Nevertheless this is not a folk-song symphony. Only three folk themes are used, the second of them as scarcely more than passing reference. Hence the opening horn tune is treated as more than a piece of atmosphere. It is a genuine folk melody, a Ukrainian variant of the Russian tune 'Down by Mother Volga' known in various forms and bearing some relation to a city song, 'O you winter, little winter', as well as to certain church chants; it was also associated with the Cossack rebel Stenka Razin, and was a favourite among students. But although Tchaikovsky seems to abandon it as soon as he has set the mood in the opening *andante sostenuto,* harmonising it with his familiar scales and little decorative string flourishes, he reintroduces it in the development and builds his movement carefully towards the moment when its return is both structurally and dramatically satisfying; the natural conclusion to the movement is a coda in which the horn once again sings the theme, over the scalic harmonisation that originally accompanied the bassoon repeat of it.

Although what Tchaikovsky calls 'the thread in the seams' is obvious not merely to 'the experienced eye' in that the transitions have a somewhat strained quality, the first subject is built on a forceful little five-note figure derived from the introduction; the more conventional and 'Western' continuation which Tchaikovsky devises for it plays little part in the development. Nor is the second subject much more than a brief phrase introduced more, one senses, for the sake of contrast than as argumentative matter. The imaginative substance of the movement rests less in the interaction of the two subjects than in the relationship of the first subject to the horn folk-song; even if the movement does tug a little at the seams, it is an original and thoughtful piece of music.

For the second movement Tchaikovsky used the bridal march from Act III of his discarded opera *Undine*: its less than jubilant nature is explained by the plot, in which the hero's wedding is repeatedly interrupted by the water-sprite's emissaries. The form is a simple ABACABA. A is the march, first delivered by clarinets in the chalumeau register and bassoons over a steady tonic-dominant drum-beat, and rescored on each appearance. B consists of a double answer, a dotted-note figure over which a graceful string melody presently enters. C is a variant of No. 6 of *Fifty Russian Folksongs,* 'Spin, O my spinner'.

EX. 6

Having ingeniously avoided a more lyrical slow movement, in which it might have been difficult not to use folk themes for their own sake and thus tilt the balance away from symphonic structure towards a piece of tone-painting as in the First Symphony, Tchaikovsky now reverts to the traditional scherzo-trio pattern. The busy scherzo occupies an area somewhere between Beethoven and Mendelssohn or still more Berlioz's 'Queen Mab'; the trio abruptly changes the rhythm from 3/8 to 2/8 with a tune that has a distinct flavour of folk-song, though even Russian scholars have not identified it as such.

The theme of the finale, however, was a very popular tune, the Ukrainian song 'Ta vnadyvsya zhuravel' ('The Crane': 'zhuravl' is also the Russian for a crane). Vladimir Stasov, in his enthusiasm for nationalist music, went so far as to call this movement a masterpiece, 'in terms of colour, *facture* and humour . . . one of the most important creations of the entire Russian school'. While it is scarcely that, Tchaikovsky does skilfully solve the notorious finale problem with a device that not only suits his talents but that comes naturally out of the thematic nature and the simplicity of method that characterise the symphony. After a *moderato* (based on 'The Crane') whose grandiose manner suggests that we are approaching this part of the Ukraine through the Great Gate of Kiev, the violins set off with an unaccompanied statement of the theme.

EX. 7

What follows is a series of variations of this elementary little four-bar phrase by orchestration and varied background alone, in the manner which Tchaikovsky had so much admired in Glinka's *Kamarinskaya*; thematically it is hardly given much contrast until a completely different theme comes in on violins, an eight-bar phrase in which, however, as balance to the very square nature of 'The Crane', the rhythm is divided as 3+3+2 – in rhythm a rumba but in spirit a Tchaikovsky waltz with a beat missing, foreshadowing the 5/4 movement of the *Pathétique*.

EX. 8

The increasingly close alternation of the two themes produces what one might call development by modulation, through a surprising cycle of keys, before a *presto* whisks the work home.

Although the Second Symphony was enthusiastically received at its first performance, in Moscow on 7 February 1873 under Nikolay Rubinstein, Tchaikovsky retained his doubts about his symphonic abilities and in 1879 revised the work and completely rewrote the first movement in the form we now know – not a change for the better, according to Taneyev. This revised version was first performed in St Petersburg on 12 February 1881 under Karl Zike. Tchaikovsky had meanwhile completed, in 1875, his Third Symphony.

Symphony No. 3 in D

The English nickname for this symphony, 'The Polish', originally fostered by Sir August Manns, is misleading. Apart from the *tempo di polacca* marking of the finale's *allegro con fuoco* there is nothing to suggest Polish influence; nor is it likely that a composer as consciously Russian as Tchaikovsky would have wasted much mourning on Poland's sorrows, as has been suggested. So far from invoking any national or folk-song influence, it is the most academic and abstract of the six. He composed it quickly, between the middle of June and the middle of August 1875; and despite professional troubles, principally the attack on his First Piano Concerto by Nikolay Rubinstein, he was able to find the peace of mind to concentrate in a congenial country atmosphere surrounded by his father and other relations. Nevertheless, the symphony lacks the individuality of its fellows; and there is a somewhat awkward tension between the regularity of symphonic form he was consciously trying to achieve in a 'Germanic' way and his own characteristics. The insertion of the *alla tedesca* is a case in point: although it balances the scherzo on the other side of the most substantial movement, the *andante elegiaco,* there is a stronger sense of the conventional four-movement pattern being interrupted by a movement which Tchaikovsky could not resist but also felt (as he did not with the Fifth Symphony) must not displace the traditional scherzo. Yet if a sacrifice had to be made, in terms of sheer quality it would be the scherzo. Its Mendelssohnian cast is less convincing than in the trio of the *alla tedesca,* where Tchaikovsky is much more at ease contrasting his waltz with chattering triplets in a manner he was to explore again when he came to write the march of his *Pathétique.*

There is an unresolved tension, too, in the nature of the thematic invention. The opening funeral march is one of Tchaikovsky's most original notions, beautifully scored and economically worked out; but despite the adumbrations of the first subject to come, there is little real connection with the bold, over-square tune that sets off with the *allegro brillante.* Tchaikovsky cannot in fact sustain it, and is quickly driven to repeating phrases in his familiar manner. This characteristic is more prominent still in the second subject which in more conventional, 'Western' hands might run as follows:

EX. 9

Instead, Tchaikovsky produces his complete melody by his folk-based device of varied repetition, and for all that it lends a personal hue to an otherwise lame progression, the result is hardly a vintage Tchaikovsky tune:

EX. 10

Tchaikovsky clearly valued his two principal subjects for the opportunities they gave him for a regular sonata movement; just as in the finale his *polacca* theme (also constructed out of repeating phrases) lends itself to developmental sections built on imitation and even to a very studiously worked fugue leading towards the final return of the over-grand tune that is the movement's other principal material.

Both the outer movements, in fact, suggest conscious striving towards a regularity of form that did not suit Tchaikovsky. The most successful movement, apart from the charming 'interlude' *alla tedesca,* is the central *andante elegiaco,* which not only takes up the sombre mood of the opening of the whole work but shows that when freed from the dictates of sonata or of bringing off a traditional finale, Tchaikovsky was well able to develop characteristic music in a free and individual manner. The broken little horn and woodwind phrases that open the movement are not merely 'answered' by the consolatory string melody: the two are brought together in an extremely subtle emotional interplay, so that when the gloomy D minor triplets theme of the opening achieves, with the last note of the movement, the major third and is joined by a soft D major chord, there is sense of consolation and peace genuinely won.

After the first performance, in Moscow on 19 November 1875 under Nikolay Rubinstein, Tchaikovsky himself told Rimsky-Korsakov that he felt that though the work did not have any very successful ideas, it did represent a step forward technically. Certainly it gave him a new confidence in handling symphonies which brought him to the brink of his greatest achievements in the form.

THE LAST THREE SYMPHONIES

Symphony No. 4 in F minor

Two years and the greatest emotional crisis of his life separate Tchaikovsky's Third Symphony from his Fourth. Towards the end of 1876 he received a commission for some arrangements from Nadezhda Filaretovna von Meck, the wealthy patroness whom by their mutual agreement he was never to meet and whose generosity allowed him to abandon the teaching he abhorred to concentrate on composition. Their correspondence has already been quoted; it was the substance of an extraordinary relationship, conducted in exaggerated terms on both sides, and one which they were wise enough not to put to the test of reality. Perhaps she fixed her emotions upon an ideal artist of the imagination, in some way kin to her own neurotic sensibility, while he found in her a semi-maternal figure; certainly he was able to confess to her, though very obliquely, the subject of the Fourth Symphony he was proposing to dedicate to her. 'Our symphony', as he calls it in his letters to her, opens with a theme representing 'a force which, like the sword of Damocles, hangs perpetually over our heads and is always embittering the soul'. He uses the same simile when writing to his brother Modest; and here he is openly referring to the fear that his homosexuality should be exposed. So anguished did he become that he took the desperate decision to marry; and when, early in 1877, like Tatyana to Eugene Onegin in the opera he was then writing, a young student named Antonina Milyukova wrote to him with a passionate declaration of love, he allowed himself to contract a marriage with her. He made no bones about his unsuitability: he hoped that a detached, merely friendly relationship would prove possible for them both, that at the very least it would stop the gossips' mouths. For all the doubts he had, which he detailed in a letter to Mme von Meck, he felt that this was another manifestation of Fate. They were married in July; within days he found the relationship insufferable. He resumed work on *Onegin* and the Fourth Symphony at Kamenka in August; joining his wife in Moscow, he suffered a further crisis and attempted suicide. His doctor urged that the only course if his reason was to be saved was immediate separation from his wife.

Out of the crisis came to Tchaikovsky, in his state of morbidly heightened sensibility, the strengthened conviction that some sinister force of fate really did threaten his life; and it was this, coupled with his need to confide his emotions to music, which shaped his Fourth Symphony and enabled him at last to discover the symphonic method which matched his temperament to his talents. When Mme von Meck wrote to him asking for a detailed account of 'our symphony', he replied with a letter admitting that the work was programmatic and was based on the idea of Beethoven's Fifth Symphony – namely, the triumph of the sensibility over the attacks of Fate.

The introduction is the *seed* of the whole symphony, beyond question the main idea. This is *Fate*, the fatal force which prevents our hopes of happiness from being realised, which watches jealously to see that our bliss and peace are not complete and unclouded, which, like the Sword of Damocles, is suspended over the head and perpetually poisons the soul. It is inescapable and it can never be overcome. One must submit to it and to futile yearnings. The gloomy, despairing feeling grows stronger and more burning. Would it not be better to turn away from reality and plunge into dreams? O, joy! at last a sweet and tender vision appears. Some bright, gracious human form passes and beckons somewhere. How delightful! how remote now sounds the obsessive first theme of the Allegro. Little by little, dreams have completely enveloped the soul. All that was gloomy, joyless is forgotten. It is here, it is here, happiness.

No! These were dreams, and *Fate* awakens us harshly. Thus, life is a perpetual alternation between grim reality and transient dreams and reveries of happiness. There is no haven. Drift upon that sea until it engulfs and submerges you in its depths. That, approximately, is the programme of the first movement.

Already in his Second Symphony Tchaikovsky had experimented with an introduction whose opening theme would return in the course of the development of the succeeding sonata move-

EX. II

24

ment. Here, however, the idea works more effectively because it is linked to a dramatic idea, the notion of Fate, rather than being a mere schematic attempt at achieving unity.

The discovery, too, that for all its problems sonata could be used to bear the weight of his emotional life enabled Tchaikovsky to develop a much stronger form. The notorious 'seams' still show, as they always would; but even the note of straining towards the next wholehearted utterance of a theme now has its dramatic point. The waltz, previously graceful contrast or light relief, is found to possess a pathos of its own as a *valse triste,* particularly as the response, opening the main section of the movement, to the hammering 'fate' theme on brass which opens the symphony. The theme is kin to the near-waltz of the Second Symphony (Ex. 8), but the hesitance of the cross-rhythms contains a proper emotional point; moreover, the downward, yielding course of the repeated figure in modified sequences, followed by its struggle upwards again, is now more than a melody, however fine, made for its own sake, but something embodying the nature of the symphony being undertaken.

EX. 12

The 'dream world' Tchaikovsky describes in his letter is, as one would expect, that of the ballet: the second subject group, with its little woodwind scales and its lulling string theme, has an artificial prettiness touchingly remote from the first theme, not properly reconcilable with it despite the skilful alternation which

Tchaikovsky devises and certainly no match for the battering of the 'fate' theme on brass which repeatedly intervenes. But even the deficiencies of Tchaikovsky's symphonic style are turned to advantage; for in the impossibility of the two working organically upon each other, each one subject to the 'fate' theme, there is an expressive dramatic point made about the composer's own inability either to find real solace in escape or to overcome the sense of a malignant force dogging his life. It is the most successful sonata movement he had yet composed; and the answer has come not out of studying to achieve 'correct' formal procedures but in the coinciding of inventive manner with emotional matter.

The middle two movements pursue this vein with images of the separateness imposed by unhappiness. Tchaikovsky has described the atmosphere of the slow movement, which he marks *andantino in modo di canzona*:

This is that melancholy feeling which comes in the evening when one sits alone, tired from work, having picked up a book but let it fall from one's hands. A whole host of memories appears. And one is sad because so much is *gone, past*, and it is pleasant to remember one's youth. . . . There were happy moments, when young blood pulsed and life was good. There were gloomy moments, too, irreplaceable losses. All that is indeed somewhere far off. And it is sad and somehow sweet to bury oneself in the past.

The melancholy mood is set with a melody on the oboe consisting of no less than twenty bars all in even quavers, with the lightest *pizzicato* accompaniment – a beautiful image of the mind wandering steadily but without any particular focus. The string answer is more positive, and decorations in the form of running scales on flute and clarinet are added before the *più mosso* middle section, a grave, remote dance initiated on clarinet and bassoon. The return of the opening theme is accompanied with little woodwind runs similar to those surrounding the 'escape' second subject of the first movement. The play of the mind in the third movement, marked *scherzo-pizzicato ostinato* is more fanciful:

It consists of capricious arabesques, elusive apparitions that pass through the imagination when one has drunk a little wine and feels the first stages of intoxication. . . . The imagination is liberated, and for some reason sets off painting strange pictures. Among them one remembers the picture of a roistering peasant and a street song. Then somewhere in the distance a military parade passes.

Again the first theme is in even quavers, but here played fast, pizzicato, and with a brilliant sense of quick-nerved imagination: apart from anything else, it is a *locus classicus* of scoring, much imitated and never excelled. The drunken peasant appears in a hectic little oboe tune, the military band in a stiff strutting theme over which fragments of the oboe tune are presently scattered, together with phrases of the pizzicato theme which then returns. All three are flung together in a brilliant free-for-all that drives the movement home hilariously.

The finale bursts in with a flourish, portraying a national festival:

If you find no cause for joy within yourself, look for it in others. Go to the people. Look, they know how to enjoy themselves, giving themselves up to undivided feelings of pleasure . . . Scarcely has one forgotten oneself and been carried away at the sight of someone else's pleasure than indefatigable *Fate* returns again and reminds you of yourself. But others pay no heed to you. . . . Reproach yourself and do not say that all the world is sad. Simple but strong joys do exist. Rejoice in others' rejoicing. To live is still bearable.

The substance of the movement thus introduced is a folk-song, 'In the fields there stood a birch', and a theme suggesting a village band, with brief connecting passages generally using the opening flourish. At the height of the rejoicing the 'fate' theme thunders in once more, *fff*; and as it softens to *p* a drooping figure in the strings seems to indicate that it has silenced the music. But the village band returns, and builds up a coda based on the two themes to whirl the symphony to its conclusion in a burst of high spirits.

Even folk-song and national atmosphere, then, are related to the central matter of the symphony instead of being treated for their own sake; as is the ballet idiom which troubled Taneyev and led him to complain that 'hearing the symphony, my inner eye sees involuntarily Mrs Sobeshchanskaya or Gillert no. 2 [ballerinas], which puts me out of humour and spoils my pleasure in the many beauties of the work'. Tchaikovsky accepted the criticism, contenting himself with the observation that he could not understand why 'ballet music' should be a term of reproach. In this symphony it is not, since it represents one side of the composer and stands for the escape world of dreams into which he would try to plunge himself. In a sense, however, the entire symphony is about escape: the pretty illusions of the first movement are dropped in favour of a different kind of daydreaming in the central pair of movements, and these in turn give way to an exteriorisation of the emotions into a generalised sense of festivity. It is not psychologically true for the temperament described in the symphony to be able to console itself enduringly in watching the happiness of simple people: Berlioz's Faust was more honest, and closer to the essential Romantic sensibility, when he found the contrast between the peasants' 'natural' contentment and his own misery an added anguish; Tchaikovsky might have noted that Olenin in *The Cossacks*, the book which he had recently chosen as a present from Tolstoy, painfully discovers it. It is more convincing when the 'fate' theme strikes across the festivity and brings the music low than when the little march begins again and is built up into a further demonstration of high spirits. One reason is that Tchaikovsky has contributed no personal element to the scene, as in the first three movements: there is no sense of anyone being involved in it until the 'fate' theme strikes. This is dismissed, not absorbed and conquered in the music. Nevertheless, however precarious the triumph, it is asserted; and in this there is a quality as near the heroic as Tchaikovsky was ever to come. If the example of Beethoven's Fifth Symphony is not carried through, it is absorbed into a symphonic experience of a kind for which Tchaikovsky was uniquely qualified. For all the defects of form which the calculating eye can, with Tchaikovsky himself, discover, he has here brought his gifts into a full relationship with each other in a genuinely subjective symphony.

Symphony No. 5 in E minor

A full decade was to elapse between the première of the Fourth Symphony in Moscow in 1878 and the composition and performance of the Fifth. They were years of recovery and of the consolidation of his reputation. By 1880, when Tchaikovsky was 40, all his completed operas had been produced and his orchestral works given performances that were sympathetically received. Abroad his fame was spreading, and he was able to work, with the interruption of almost a year in 1880–1, either at his sister's estate at Kamenka or on his various travels. 'The Tchaikovsky of 1885', wrote his brother Modest, 'seemed a new man compared with the nervous and misanthropic Tchaikovsky of 1878.' He settled first at Maidanovo, near Klin on the road between Moscow and St

Petersburg, then moved into a smaller house nearby and took up a regular routine of work. His confidence was strong enough for him to embark upon a European tour in 1888 that even included engagements as a conductor; though he managed to overcome his earlier panic about conducting, he remained to the end doubtful about his powers. His diary for these travels describes his encounters with Brahms, Grieg and other musicians of the day; there is a vivid sketch of Nikisch working with the Gewandhaus Orchestra. The candour and good humour with which he records the hostile criticism he encountered, together with the modesty of his comments on the favourable opinions he won, show how different a man he was from the tortured, neurotic figure who had been brought so low by the reception of his early works and the disasters of 1876. Back in Russia by the end of 1888, he settled in a new house near Klin (now admirably maintained as a museum, with all his music, furniture and personal belongings). From here he wrote to Nadezhda von Meck:

I cannot tell you what a pleasure it has been to watch my flowers grow and see daily – even hourly – new blossoms coming out. When I am quite old and past composing I shall devote myself to growing flowers. Meanwhile, I have been working with good results, for half the symphony is now orchestrated.

Although he had confided the content of his Fourth Symphony in some detail to Mme von Meck, he always believed that explicitness was unnecessary. Yet for the new symphony he roughed out a brief programme for the first movement before starting on the work:

Introduction. Complete resignation before Fate, or, which is the same, before the inscrutable predestination of Providence. Allegro (i) Murmurs, doubts, plaints, reproaches against xxx. (ii) Shall I throw myself in the embraces of faith ???

Even this note gives a clue to the nature of the Fifth Symphony. Whether or not XXX represents an actual person, it seems certain that he is referring to his central emotional problem, his homosexuality (elsewhere in the diary mentioned cryptically as Z or *This*). 'Complete resignation' suggests that he had come to terms with his nature, that Fate is no longer something to be struggled against nor even (in spite of what he says) to be regarded in quite the same light as Providence: the new term implies the more philosophical, even religious, acceptance which his final comment

supports. Though not strictly pious, Tchaikovsky was in some
way a believer, certainly one with a strong artistic feeling for the
Orthodox liturgy. 'My mind obstinately refuses to be convinced
by dogma', he once wrote to Nadezhda von Meck, adding later,
'On the other hand, my education and the ingrained habits of
childhood, combined with the poetry contained in the story of
Christ and His teaching, all persuade me in spite of myself to turn
to Him with prayers when I am sad, with gratitude when I am
happy.' However he may have answered his own question to himself, there is a comparative, if precarious, peace of mind reflected
in this symphony. 'The intelligent man who believes in God', he
wrote to Nadezhda von Meck on another occasion, 'has a shield
against which the blows of fate are absolutely vain.'

The Providence theme of the work is hence of a very different
order from the battering brass motive associated with Fate in the
Fourth Symphony:

EX. 13

This is both characteristic and ingenious. It has Tchaikovsky's
melodic fingerprints – the simple figure immediately repeated a
third higher, the phrase completed by two similar scales. But the
opening pair of bars also has a rhythmic identity which will allow
it to be used and recognised even when played purely as a rhythm,
as in the finale; and the harmony implied is the plain tonic-sub-

dominant alternation which is in fact the basis of the movement, imparting a plagal flavour which matches the mood of resignation. The same simple tonic-subdominant alternation of chords accompanies the first subject of the *allegro con anima,* a jerky little 6/8 tune first heard on clarinets and bassoons that could well represent the 'murmurs', just as the answers and the ensuing *ff* and *fff* outbursts might be the 'doubts, plaints and reproaches', and the sudden *piano* and the tender rising string figure with its delicate woodwind answer the 'embraces of faith' – though as Tchaikovsky was always at pains to emphasise, it is misleading to attempt too precise an identification of his meanings.

Tchaikovsky left no further explicit clues to the course of the symphony; though it has been reported that over the horn melody which opens the slow movement he wrote the words, 'O, que je t'aime! O, mon amie! O, how I love . . . If you love me . . . With desire and passion . . .' The tune is marked *dolce con molto espressione,* the movement itself *andante cantabile, con alcuna licenza*; there are hardly more than three or four bars at a time in the first section without some tempo alteration – *animando, ritenuto, sostenuto, animando, sostenuto, con moto, animato* and so forth, repeatedly, both with the main tune and its important oboe subsidiary. The atmosphere is one of tenderness and yearning, always growing to new pitches of intensity, that seem to be on the verge of breaking into articulate speech. The calm of the first movement has been replaced by a passionate outpouring of emotion that is not stemmed by the *moderato con anima* section in which woodwind utter a curious little four-bar phrase that is richly developed until suddenly the 'Providence' theme breaks in *fff*, this time carrying a strong feeling of hostile fate. The movement is resumed with the horn theme on violins, to a gentle oboe counter-melody, but the emotional tension quickly mounts once more to the feverish climax of the passage around Ex. 5. The 'Providence' theme breaks in again; and this time the climax is followed by a few broken, sorrowfully falling phrases. When the Tempo I is resumed, the secondary theme is played *dolcissimo* on strings over pulsing horns and bassoons, and in this wistful mood the movement ends. Whether or not Tchaikovsky did set the quoted words over his opening horn melody, the whole piece bears the feeling of a deeply felt, tragic love scene, frustrated by fate. There is not bitterness, nor even despair, but a sense that the 'complete resignation before fate' has been reasserted.

By previous example, the world of the ballet was Tchaikovsky's escape into a dream world. The waltz which follows is elegant but its quietly plaintive falling phrases and feminine endings produce much less sense of a back being turned on reality than, for instance, with the second subject of the Fourth Symphony's opening movement. (It is related to a street song which the composer took down from a boy in Florence and used complete in his song 'Pimpinella', Op. 38, No. 6.) This gives way to a curious syncopated theme on bassoon, joined by flutes and clarinets, before a sprightly little *spiccato* figure of running scales that acts as trio section. But even here the mood is not so decorative as in passages that appear to be similar; only for a brief spell are the graver chords of the accompaniment abandoned for pure lightness, and gradually the waltz reasserts itself. There is only one appearance from the 'Providence' theme, very softly on low clarinets and bassoons as if as a reminder, and the movement ends with half a dozen cheerful chords.

With the finale Tchaikovsky returns to sonata form; but the two principal subjects – a forceful, rhythmic chordal theme with a more nervous oboe answer, and an easily flowing woodwind phrase – are less the matter of the movement than the establishment of the 'Providence' theme as no longer threatening or even something requiring resignation but triumphantly absorbed. The movement sets off with an *andante maestoso* statement of the 'Providence' theme in the major; this returns to open the development section still more confidently; and the end of the recapitulation builds up on rhythmic references to it towards a dramatic ritenuto and a pause. The coda, *moderato assai e molto maestoso,* is triumphant: marching chords and grandiose woodwind scales introduce Providence in a *largamente* statement to a powerful brass counterpoint, building up strongly towards a *presto,* based on the oboe answer to the first subject and on the second subject; and with the final *molto meno mosso* the opening first subject of the movement returns in a majestic trumpet fanfare, *ffff*.

There remains something unconvincing in this triumph. It is not that Tchaikovsky has mishandled his motto theme, for its returns throughout the work are judged with dramatic, almost operatic, skill – the formidable interruptions in the slow movement, the softer reminder in the waltz. Nor can the criticism be levelled against him, as it can over the Fourth Symphony, that he has dodged the issue of assimilating his 'fate' or 'Providence' theme musically. Yet however effective his placing of the theme in the finale, especially his preparation at the end of the recapitulation for the coda, there is something too easy about it. Coming so soon after the sad tenderness of the waltz, when the 'Providence' theme is still an intervention and carries a hint of warning, this major-key confidence seems too lightly won. What has transpired, one asks, to alter the issue of resignation before Providence so completely? The final statement of the theme, with rhythms pounding and brass blaring, has a bombast of a kind Tchaikovsky rarely sank to, and only in works such as the *1812* overture which he cordially despised. Until the finale, the symphony has embodied a nature fundamentally unhappy but brought into a state of equilibrium. Now for the first time a note of falseness, of overstatement, enters into the music; and although it is all bravely carried through, the final triumph cannot help seeming hollow. Tchaikovsky himself developed doubts about the work:

I have become convinced that this symphony is unsuccessful. There is something repulsive about it, a certain excess of gaudiness and insincerity, artificiality. And the public instinctively recognises this. . . . Yesterday evening I looked through the Fourth Symphony, *ours*! What a difference, how much superior and better it is! Yes, this is very, very sad!

Symphony No. 6 in B minor (Pathétique)

By his last years, Tchaikovsky had organised his days at Klin into a settled routine of work. He would rise between seven and eight, drink tea and read the Bible in the sunny little alcove adjoining his music room, and begin work punctually at half-past nine: inspiration, he once said in a letter, is a guest who only comes to those who invite her. He would work on until one, take an afternoon walk during which he thought out ideas and made notes, work again from five until seven, talk or play the piano till eleven, when he would go to bed. He seldom deviated from this programme by more than a minute or so, his brother Modest records. Yet though the meticulousness of his routine is reflected in the efficiency of his working processes – the sketches for his last symphony are rapidly scribbled and remarkably close to the finished score – it gives no clue to the emotional turmoil and despair in the music. Not even to Modest would he divulge the meaning behind the work. The most he would admit was contained in a letter to his beloved nephew 'Bob' Davidov at the time he was planning the work:

At the time of my journey I had an idea for another symphony, this time with a programme, but a programme of a kind that will remain an enigma to all – let them guess, but the symphony will just be called *Programme Symphony* (*No. 6*); *Symphonie à Programme* (*No. 6*); *Eine Programm Symphonie* (*No. 6*). This programme is permeated with subjective feeling, and quite often on my journey, composing it in my mind, I wept copiously. When I reached home, I settled down to the sketches, and the work went with such ardour and at such speed that in less than four days I had completely finished the first movement and clearly outlined the remaining movements in my head. Half the third movement is already done. Formally there will be much that is new in this symphony, and incidentally the Finale won't be a loud Allegro but, on the contrary, a very slow-moving Adagio. You can't imagine what bliss I feel in the conviction that my time is not yet over and that work is still possible. Of course I may be wrong, but I don't think so.

By the end of August he was writing again to Davidov:

I can tell you in all sincerity that I consider this symphony the best thing I have ever done. In any case, it is the most deeply felt. And I love it as I have never loved any of my compositions.

Only after the first performance on 16 October did Tchaikovsky give further thought to the question of a title, before dispatching the score to his publisher. Modest called upon him and found him dissatisfied with a mere 'No. 6' for so personal a work, hardly any more enthusiastic about 'Programme Symphony', since he refused to make the programme public. Modest's first suggestion, 'Tragic', was rejected; his afterthought was accepted, and so the work has come down to us as the 'Pathetic'. Particularly for an Englishman, it is a misleading title: the French 'Pathétique' and the Russian 'Patetichesky' derived from it carry a closer feeling of the original Greek 'pathos', also distorted in English usage and really meaning 'suffering'.

The nature of the suffering has remained undisclosed. Certainly Tchaikovsky was at the time much obsessed with death; though he had no premonition of his own death on 6 November from cholera, he had recently lost three close friends, and he quotes in the course of the first movement a phrase characteristic of the Orthodox funeral service ('With the Saints'). He was brought low by the break with Nadezhda von Meck, whose letters he often re-read and with whom he had gone some way towards effecting a reconciliation. According to Modest, he was attempting 'to exorcise and drive out the sombre demons that had so long plagued him'.

It is, nevertheless, a symphony of defeat. As in the preceding symphonies, the introduction gives the key to the nature of the whole work. In No. 4 the 'fate' theme was a brusque battering, devoid in its first statement of any humanising harmony; in No. 5 the quieter 'Providence' theme was given a tonic-subdominant harmony, a repeated plagal cadence; here the despair is evident in the theme itself, with its painful efforts to heave itself up and its final failure to do so, as well as in the slow chromatic decline of the harmony, and the sombre scoring for bassoon over divided violas and double basses.

EX. 14

The theme of the *allegro non troppo* is derived from this; but for all the energy of the figuration there is no sense of gaiety, and at all turns and with many variants the harmony maintains the down-ward chromatic progress. The second-subject group leads off with one of Tchaikovsky's most famous tunes, cast in the same desperate, impassioned vein as Ex. 5 and played on muted strings over grumbling brass and wind chords; the marking is *teneramente, molto cantabile, con espansione,* with the familiar alterations of impetus every couple of bars – *andante, incalzando, ritenuto, come prima, ritenuto.* The answer is a lighter flute and bassoon theme in rising scales; but here again the melody falls back on itself, and is answered by a more obviously sorrowful descending figure. The *andante* theme returns with greater passion, but declines into virtual silence – *pppppp.* The development opens with a crash: this is some of the most violent music Tchaikovsky ever wrote, developing the opening theme in a furious string passage openly marked *feroce* and only dying down from the full orchestral outburst to admit the Orthodox funeral theme *cantabile.* But this meets with a shrill, even mocking answer, and the opening theme returns in troubled fragments. In none of his symphonies did Tchaikovsky handle his development so forcefully; not only has he brought his symphonic language to its highest pitch of mastery, but he is able to base it on a theme that is at once emotionally expressive and technically adaptable to symphonic development. So powerful is the impetus that this section carries on beyond its own formal bounds into a curious passage built on the descending scales and a falling semitone figure pounded out on brass; the recapitulation can thus be brief, and is confined to the second subject, now *con dolcezza* over a climbing scale accompaniment. But this too sinks into near-silence over a muttering accompaniment, and the short coda is to the heavy downward tread of pizzicato scales. In a sense it is the same battle being waged as in the two previous symphonies; but where first there was resistance and secondly acceptance, of a kind, now there is defeat.

Even the waltz to which Tchaikovsky now turns is no longer consolation or escape; for by a stroke of genius it is in 5/4, a broken-backed waltz, limping yet graceful, serving the purpose of dramatic contrast to the grimness of the first movement in Tchaikovsky's familiar manner, yet unable to achieve the natural momentum of dance. He had experimented with a *Valse à cinq temps* at much the same time, as No. 16 of the *18 Morceaux* (Op. 72); but the somewhat mechanical nimbleness of that 5/8 vivace has much less of his own peculiar grace with waltzes. No subtleties of harmony are needed when so much is contained in this touching 5/4 melody, with its second strain in which the two-bar phrases are constantly varied as a means of keeping the tune moving yet unable to break out of its limited circle: a method skilfully reduced to a one-bar formula for a trio that reinforces the mood and the point while acting as effective contrast. Nothing in principle could be simpler than this minuet-and-trio form with its brief, and scarcely more menacing, coda; yet it too is in its way the consummation of Tchaikovsky's art in knowing himself, in understanding how even his love of dance forms could at last be brought into a symphonic experience.

The march which follows is no less skilful. In the context of the symphony, it might be expected to be either a funeral march or perhaps an outburst of manic hilarity pressing towards the edge of reason. Tchaikovsky is subtler. The first part of the movement is all preparation for something – brilliant triplet figuration passed between strings and woodwind with little wisps of a theme thrown in and then abandoned, the downward scales that are the essence of the symphony only lightly touched upon, until at the right dramatic moment a rising scale on clarinets leads into the full statement of the tune that has been so cunningly prepared. This proves to be Ex. 4. On the face of it, this is a jaunty little march; but as ever with Tchaikovsky, conscious as he was of melody, of the lyrical idea, as the essence of his music, there is more in it than at first meets the ear. The intervals are almost entirely cold fourths; the ceaseless triplets become a descending scale in the accompaniment, and the second half of the tune itself is also a decorated descent whose last-minute attempt to rise high meets with an overthrow in a rush of notes. This is the whole substance of a brilliantly sustained movement that drives towards ever greater tension without ever developing the mood or enriching itself, until finally it reaches the limits of orchestral excitement and is spent.

It is unquestionably a thrilling movement, but there is a frigidity at its heart which is explained when the dreadful grief of the final *adagio lamentoso* falls upon the ear. The opening theme (divided between first and second violins) is the same descending scale that has lain within so much of the symphony's invention; when the strings struggle up to a climax by much the same heaving process as at the very opening of the entire work, the wind drag

37

TCHAIKOVSKY SYMPHONIES AND CONCERTOS

the music down across two octaves in a scalic melody twisting painfully upon itself. The central *andante* section, over a softly beating horn pedal, begins with a gentler melody marked *con lenezza e devozione*. Once again it is formed out of a segment of a descending scale; with more sustained effort than in any of the symphony's previous themes it builds up to a tremendous *fff* climax, maintains itself for a few bars, and then is overthrown in a rush of scales down to a shattering chord and silence. When it resumes, the harmony is more bitter, the opening theme more tense still; and the succeeding climaxes are violent and despairing. The outcome is a passage of solemn chords on trombones and tuba over a soft gong stroke; the second theme returns with more anguish and its sequences finally die slowly away over the steady throb of double basses into silence.

The thematic substance of the symphony, then, is a melodic figure that against its natural descending inclination lifts itself up to a climax, and then falls (or is felled); coupled with this is the descending scale accompaniment that opens the whole work and becomes the dominant feature of the finale. Into his melodic material Tchaikovsky has built the image of decline which is the matter of the work; the lyrical idea, so far from being self-sufficient or requiring careful adaptation to a set of imposed formal demands, is now genuinely the generative material of a long and extremely subtle expressive structure. Scalic figures had always been a feature of his style; so had graceful or sparkling woodwind patterns; so had dance rhythms and their feelings of contrast with reality: these characteristics, and much else in his musical language, have without any fundamental change become organic. The final defeat is foreshadowed in the very opening of this symphony as the outcome is not in the Fourth or Fifth. Clearly the emotional problem which Tchaikovsky claimed to have turned successfully away from in the Fourth Symphony and resigned himself to in the Fifth has not let him be; and there is a unity in his last symphony which shows that he really has at last acknowledged the truth of his condition, the tragedy of a passionate and tender nature doomed to frustration and guilt. However bitter the triumph, he produced out of this his greatest symphony.

THE CONCERTOS

Piano Concerto No. 1 in B flat minor

Tchaikovsky's six symphonies cover almost his entire working life, from 1866, when he was 26, to the year of his death, 1893; and they represent both the course of his most intimate emotional life and his flowering as a craftsman. The concertos cover a narrower span, from the First Piano Concerto of 1875 to the Third of 1893; and while they are no less individual or finely wrought, they occupy a more limited emotional range. Yet the first of them all, the B flat minor Piano Concerto, is on the scale of Tchaikovsky's mature symphonies; and despite its enduring popularity above all Tchaikovsky's other concert works, it has caused a certain amount of puzzlement – most notoriously before it was even orchestrated, as Tchaikovsky himself recorded in a long letter to Nadezhda von Meck:

> In December 1874 I had written a Piano Concerto! Not being a pianist, I considered it necessary to consult a virtuoso as to any points in my Concerto which might be technically impracticable, ungrateful or ineffective. I had need of a severe critic, but at the same time one friendlily disposed towards me.

The obvious choice was Nikolay Rubinstein (although Tchaikovsky had some misgivings about him); and on Christmas Eve Tchaikovsky met him and a former fellow-student, Nikolay Hubert, at the Moscow Conservatoire.

> I played the first movement. Not a single word, not a single remark! If you knew how stupid and intolerable is the situation of a man who cooks and sets before a friend a meal, which he proceeds to eat in silence! Oh for one word, for friendly attack, but for God's sake one word of sympathy, even if not of praise. Rubinstein was amassing his storm. ... Above all, I did not want sentence on the artistic aspect. My need was for remarks about the virtuoso piano technique. R's eloquent silence was of the greatest significance. He seemed to be saying: 'My friend, how can I speak of detail when the whole thing is antipathetic?' I fortified myself with patience and played through to the end. Still silence. I stood up and asked, 'Well?' Then a torrent poured from Nikolay Grigoryevich's mouth, gentle at first, then more and more growing into the sound of a Jupiter Tonans. It turned out that my concerto was worthless and unplayable; passages were so fragmented, so clumsy, so badly written that they were beyond rescue; the work itself was bad, vulgar; in places I had stolen from other composers; only two or three pages were worth preserving; the rest must be thrown away or completely rewritten. 'Here, for instance, this – now what's all that?' (he caricatured my music on

the piano) 'And this? How could anyone . . .' etc, etc. The chief thing I can't
reproduce is the *tone* in which all this was uttered. In a word, a disinterested
person in the room might have thought I was a maniac, a talentless, senseless
hack who had come to submit his rubbish to an eminent musician.

Speechless with anger and dismay, Tchaikovsky left and went up-
stairs. Rubinstein followed him, and seeing how distressed he was
attempted more gently to point out what he believed to be the
work's faults: if certain alterations could be made, he added, he
would play the concerto in public. But Tchaikovsky was on his
mettle, and refused to alter a single note. He struck out the original
dedication to Taneyev and substituted one to the highly flattered
Hans von Bülow, whom he knew to be an admirer of his music.
Bülow gave the first performance in the course of an American
concert tour, in Boston in 1875. Not for four years was the breach
with Rubinstein healed; and the move then came with Rubinstein's
admission that he had been completely in the wrong and his
promise, faithfully kept, to study the work and play it.

So popular is the concerto that it may seem difficult now to
understand the reasons for Rubinstein's objections. They really
fall into three categories – that is, if we accept Tchaikovsky's probably over-dramatised account to Nadezhda von Meck. Firstly,
he thought the piano writing 'manufactured and clumsy'. Tchaikovsky was no virtuoso, and as well as passages (such as the famous
quadruple octaves) which have been known to fell the greatest
pianists, there are certainly sections where effects playable only
with great effort are almost covered by the orchestra. It is difficult
writing of a kind that the very professional Rubinstein might be
excused for finding merely perverse when he had insufficiently
penetrated the style and necessities of the music. Secondly, he
found the invention both second-hand and second-rate. It is hard
to see whose influence Rubinstein had in mind; as to the actual
quality of the material, he was perfectly right in thinking it uneven,
though as so often this would seem more strikingly so at a first
hearing. Thirdly, he seems to have been baffled by the work as a
whole. To a brilliant but conservative musician in the Russia of
1874 it must indeed have seemed unorthodox. Not only are there,
in addition to the pianistic details that troubled Rubinstein, some
awkwardnesses of the kind Tchaikovsky himself acknowledged
when referring to the 'seams' of his forms; there is the oddity of

the work's opening, the blatant but well-loved tune which after a horn summons is sung on violins and cellos over dramatically crashing piano chords. The work is in B flat minor, but begins in its own relative major, D flat: this is surprising enough, but would be explicable in the light of Tchaikovsky's fondness in his symphonies for beginning with an introduction in slower tempo, to be reintroduced in the succeeding sonata movement (as in the Second and Third Symphonies) or as statement of a motto theme which will permeate the entire work (as in the Fourth and Fifth Symphonies, and to a much subtler extent in the Sixth). However, neither as motto nor as ingredient in any form does anything from this section recur: not even in similarity of manner does it ever return again. Conceivably Tchaikovsky originally meant it to do so, perhaps capping the entire work in the 'triumphant' style of the finale of the Fifth Symphony, and having found a different solution by then could not bring himself to abandon an idea of which he was proud. It is difficult to see how the passage could be removed, for the work would open weakly on the unprepared statement of the *allegro con spirito,* and not even those who least care for this side of Tchaikovsky could seriously wish the introduction to be dropped. As it stands, it is a grandiose gesture that announces the entry into a virtuoso piano concerto of handsome proportions and tuneful content.

The first subject of the movement proper is supposed to be one of the borrowed themes that make their appearances in the work, in this case a Ukrainian folk-tune. Broken up as it is by Tchaikovsky into rapid toccata-like triplet figuration, it shows no signs of either folk-style nor even singability: its principal function seems to be to generate the most brilliant and pianistic side of the invention in contrast to the song-like qualities of the second subject. This consists of two quite distinct elements. One, ingeniously foreshadowed before the first subject has fully run its course, is a melody in Tchaikovsky's most poignant vein; the second, re-calling the similar answer to the main love theme in the *Romeo and Juliet* overture is a gently rocking string figure. The latter proves to be close enough to the first subject to make the double subject of a large orchestral exposition; the former is reserved for piano alone, exploding out of the orchestral climax in a torrent of quadruple octaves. Formally and dramatically – which is as so often much the same in Tchaikovsky – it is a satisfying scheme, and whatever Rubinstein's doubts it makes for one of Tchaikovsky's most powerful sonata movements, a genuine musical working out of virtuoso and expressive elements.

The *andantino semplice* maintains this balance by combining within itself slow movement and scherzo. The opening theme, over a steady pulse on muted plucked strings, is a gentle flute melody:

EX. 15

It contains an inconsistency, in that the piano reply and all subsequent statements take the alternative high B flat; and this has led various conductors to alter the flute version on the assumption that Tchaikovsky simply made a mistake. However, he had ample time to make the change; and he is hardly likely to have stuck to his refusal to Rubinstein 'to alter a single note' quite so literally. Although the second version is melodically stronger, this in itself is no argument for the change: indeed, there is a certain charm in the way in which the small improvement to the tune is left to the piano. It has something in common with the searing love tune of the Fifth Symphony, though here the mood is gentle, reflective and untroubled; possibly it refers to the composer's brief engagement to the French singer Désirée Artôt in the winter of 1868–9, for the *prestissimo* section is based on a fragment of one of her songs:

EX. 16

This bears no relationship to the subject of the *andantino*, nor to the undulating little woodwind countersubject that follows; but, more mindful of his formal obligations than Rubinstein supposed,

Tchaikovsky makes an ingenious connection between the two sections of the movement by linking them with a piano figure which at once answers the flute melody and serves as a brilliant *scherzando* when played *prestissimo* to set off the middle section.

The finale is again in sonata form, based on a vigorous Russian dance that is in fact a Ukrainian song, 'Come, come Ivanka', and a serene string melody that comes in over a piano development of the first tune. More than in the first movement, there is a sharper alternation of brusque orchestral and solo statements; but the working out is again subtly devised to make musical reason of their most virtuoso elements.

Piano Concerto No. 2 in G

By 1879 the First Piano Concerto was so well set on its career of popularity, encouraged by the performances in which Nikolay Rubinstein made handsome amends for his initial attitude, that Tchaikovsky was able to write to Nadezhda von Meck in October of the new piano concerto he had begun:

> I want to dedicate it to N. G. Rubinstein in recognition of his magnificent playing of my First Concerto and of my Sonata, which left me in utter rapture after he performed it for me in Moscow.

This was in November; he had begun work while staying with his sister at Kamenka a month previously, as he told Mme von Meck:

> I am now more than ever convinced that I cannot live for long without working. A few days ago I began to sense in my spirit a kind of indefinable dissatisfaction with myself, which little by little was beginning to turn into boredom ... I realised that what I was lacking was work, and so I began to work a little. Immediately the boredom vanished, and I felt lighter in spirit. I have begun to write a piano concerto. I shall work without haste, without strain, and absolutely without tiring myself.

At first he limited himself to working in the mornings only, so keen was he to avoid the tension that had surrounded the writing of some of his other symphonic works. Further letters to Nadezhda von Meck show that he finished the finale in Paris that December before turning to the *andante*; the second half of the latter movement gave him special pleasure. After a brief interruption he returned to the completion and orchestration of the new concerto, and back in St Petersburg by March he was able to report:

> I tremble at the thought of the criticisms I may again hear from Nikolay Grigorevich, to whom this concerto is dedicated. Still, even if once more he does criticise yet nevertheless goes on to perform it brilliantly as with the First Concerto, I won't mind. It would be nice, though, if on this occasion the period between the criticism and the performance were shorter. In the meantime I am very pleased and self-satisfied about this concerto, but what lies ahead – I cannot say.

All was well, however, as Tchaikovsky told his publisher Jürgenson in August:

> In the spring I sent Rubinstein the concerto and asked him to give me his comments after he had played it and to let Taneyev change as many details of the piano part as he wished without touching the essentials of which, *no matter how much I was advised, I wouldn't change a single bar.* Taneyev wrote and told me that *there was absolutely nothing to be changed.*

Rubinstein's reaction to Tchaikovsky himself was this time understandably cautious: he suggested very tactfully that perhaps the piano part was rather episodic and too much engaged in dialogue with the orchestra rather than occupying the foreground – 'but as I say all this having scarcely played the concerto once through, perhaps I am wrong'. Tchaikovsky rejected the criticisms, but without the least rancour; indeed, when he heard the news of Rubinstein's sudden death in Paris in March 1881 he was shattered and immediately travelled there for the funeral. The first performance was now entrusted to Taneyev, who gave it in Moscow on 30 March 1882. To criticisms made at the time that the work was too long Tchaikovsky replied wryly agreeing, adding that he wished that those who had been so free with their comments earlier had suggested this at the time. He did sanction three small cuts; others, plus some revisions which greatly annoyed Tchaikovsky, were made by Ziloti for the first published edition, chiefly for the sake of simplifying the work.

If the melodic profusion of the First Piano Concerto – so great that Tchaikovsky could afford to jettison his largest tune altogether – puts the form of the complete work at risk, it remains true that he could only construct at all on a large scale on the basis of 'the lyrical idea'. With the Second Piano Concerto he was, as he reports, impelled less by some personal state of mind than by an unmotivated creative itch; and although this general sense of malaise at not working was the initiation of some of his best music, in the case of the Second Piano Concerto it seems to have led him into more routine forms of thought. The opening subject of the entire work is a grand gesture, but there is in it less of the lyrical idea than a theme well framed not only for the piano sonorities that crash out in the solo's reply to the orchestra but also for developments based on reiteration of a simple figure, in Tchaikovsky's familiar manner. The second subject is more lyrical, and ingeniously devised in two strains lying across first wind and then piano. There is again a note of contrivance, of the lyrical idea being sought for a purpose rather than occurring and then becoming the starting-point of form. It is this, no doubt, which accounts for the length of the movement: however skilfully Tchaikovsky develops these two themes, however ingeniously he alternates piano and orchestra in extended passages and deploys his themes across this span, there is a sense of largeness being sought, rather than required by the nature of the music. Of his expertise in manipulating the movement there is little question: for instance, he introduces a third theme which seems to belong in the regions of display but which comes to serve a proper formal purpose in turning the music back towards the first subject. Nevertheless, he is led to embark upon a larger structure than his ideas naturally support.

A few bars of modulation introduce the *andante non troppo*. Even in the various mutilations to which it has been subjected, this movement is virtually a triple concerto; violin and cello solo are set in equal prominence to the piano against the orchestra, and in Tchaikovsky's original it is the violin which leads in the song-like main melody over a very simple string accompaniment. It is joined by the cello before the piano makes its entry. The central part of the movement brings the piano into the more conventional role of supplying ornate figuration to accompany the theme on the orchestra; but solo violin and cello take over prominence again, and in the closing part of the movement – the section which Tchaikovsky himself particularly liked – the piano rejoins them as if moving back among its favoured companions before a coda built on a softly reiterated phrase on the orchestra over tremolo strings and arpeggiated piano chords.

The finale is an ingenious and witty combination of sonata and rondo. However, it differs from the form usually known as sonata-rondo, in which three sections corresponding to the exposition, development and recapitulation of a sonata movement are separated by two episodes. Here the feeling is more strongly of rondo, with the second subject acting as an episode; this is caused partly by the rapidity with which events succeed one another, but still more by the fact that the development concentrates on the second subject exclusively, leaving the first to sound like the return of a rondo theme when it arrives in the recapitulation. But lively as it is, the movement hardly balances the *andante* emotionally, still less the sprawling first movement formally. For all the charm of the slow movement and sparkle of the finale, indeed for all that the opening movement contains some fine and characteristic music, the concerto lacks the sense of emotional cohesion which the First Piano Concerto, despite its unevennesses, certainly maintains.

Piano Concerto No. 3 in E flat, Op. 75; Andante and Finale, Op. 79

In the spring of 1892 Tchaikovsky began a new symphony; but becoming dissatisfied with his work as symphonic material, he shortly abandoned the scheme. The music has been reconstructed as his 'seventh symphony' but cannot pass as such. Tchaikovsky himself reworked some of the material into his Third Piano Concerto (Op. 75), and an *Andante and Finale* (Op. 79) were left in short score, with no positive indication that they were destined for a concerto. However, they belonged originally to sketches for one work, and acting on the assumption that Tchaikovsky meant to keep them as such, Taneyev later rewrote the *andante* and the finale so as to complete a concerto whose opus number is thus both 75 and 79. Perhaps Tchaikovsky would have abandoned the finale, which is undistinguished, and added new movements to his preserved first: what survives is a reconstruction in concerto form of some music Tchaikovsky was planning, not a genuine Tchaikovsky piano concerto.

As far as his own first movement is concerned, there is little sign of adaptation from purely orchestral material. The piano figuration is natural, and though there are passages where this fills hardly more than a decorative role while the orchestra pursues broad melodies that could well stand on their own, this is not out of Tchaikovsky's style in the piano concertos. For the most part the music appears to have been conceived in terms as equal between piano and orchestra as in the other concertos – indeed often a good deal more so than in the Second Concerto. The second subject, a broad G major theme *cantabile ed espressivo,* fits with perfect ease onto the keyboard, with the string statement that was probably the original form standing well as its answer. The cadenza is on the scale of those in the Second Concerto's first movement, but is skilfully timed in the development section of this well-reasoned symphonic movement. The whole impression is of material re-thought in new terms rather than merely arranged for a different medium. Wise after the event, we may suppose that Tchaikovsky quickly realised that, particularly after the Fourth and Fifth Symphonies, this was not material of sufficient stature nor of adequately personal and dramatic impulse to stand as a symphony. The revision was quickly done – between 5 and 13 July 1893 – but with little pleasure; a note on the manuscript reads. 'The end, God be thanked!' He did not score it until the autumn.

When Taneyev took over, he reduced the scoring of the *andante* to woodwind, horns and strings, reserving the return of the full orchestra for the finale – an intelligent plan, carried out with a care for Tchaikovskian scoring that at times veers towards parody. The *andante* is a straightforward song-like movement, with a dialogue introduced in the central section between cello solo and piano that is handled in a very convincing Tchaikovskian vein. The movement is far more successful than the finale, a quasi-martial *allegro maestoso* that could scarcely have been the summing-up of a symphony and does little in this role for a concerto. The kindest response to it is to remember that Tchaikovsky himself abandoned it. Taneyev was being over-pious: much the best solution to the problem of what to do with the music is to perform the Third Concerto as Tchaikovsky left it, in one movement; it could with advantage be heard sometimes in concerts at which soloists wish to add something less than another full-scale concerto to the main work in their programme.

Concert Fantasia, Op. 56

There is an added reason for this solution in that Tchaikovsky himself had already composed a concertante work that is less than a full-scale concerto in his *Concert Fantasia* of 1884 (Op. 56); and to the suggestion that the concerto movement, Op. 75, was never intended to stand by itself, there is the answer that the composer was very much in two minds about the Fantasia's final version. It consists of two movements. The first is entitled 'Quasi Rondo', the *quasi* being justified by a formal layout in which the rondo matter returns only once, at the end, after a single episode. Moreover, it is modified on its return almost as if a sonata recapitulation, with the second subject reappearing in the tonic, G, instead of the dominant, D, as at first. The middle section, at the same tempo but marked *molto capriccioso e rubato,* is for piano solo: it has the manner of a cadenza, but is based on new material. The movement is thus neither sonata nor rondo, nor indeed any other textbook form: Tchaikovsky is trying out, with a high degree of success, an original method of developing ideas within the demands of piano virtuosity and orchestral accompaniment.

However, he seems thereafter to have faltered in his intentions. To this design he added, as appendix in the score, a coda consisting of a dozen pages of rather factitious brilliance that he directed should be played only if the second movement of the Fantasia were to be left out. This movement was a refugee from the Third Orchestral Suite (Op. 55), which it was originally intended to open; but Tchaikovsky carried over into the new work his doubts about the quality of the piece. In the Fantasia it is entitled 'Contrasts', and like the opening movement it solves a formal problem simply and well. There are two main themes, a slow melodic line over strumming arpeggio chords on the first two beats of a 4/2 bar (it is a natural theme for the cello counter-melody that immediately follows), and a faster theme, not unlike a Russian dance, in 2/4. These are contrastable not only in alternation but simultaneously, the second fitting four bars into one of the first. Though there are various minor episodes, the burden of the movement is the ingenious contact of the two themes, and Tchaikovsky manages the device with great liveliness. It is hard to see why he kept up his dislike of the movement; and indeed hard to see why the work has not made more than very occasional appearances in concerto programmes.

Pieces for Violin and Orchestra

In January 1875 Tchaikovsky met, at Nicholas Rubinstein's house, the young violinist Leopold Auer. Asked by Auer for a piece, he wrote in a few weeks the *Sérénade mélancolique* (Op. 26), for violin and orchestra; the first performance, however, was given by Adolf Brodsky on 28 January 1876 in Moscow. Auer did not play it until 18 November of that year. Its title describes it well. After a brief orchestral introduction, the violin enters with a wistful song-like theme over plucked lower strings and tolling horns. (The horns play a distinctive part in the piece, adding a solo against the violin at one point, and returning with a soft ostinato figure under the theme emphasising a Berliozian flattened sixth.) There is a slightly more agitated middle section before the return of the first theme with tremolo flutes now replacing horns over the same plucked bass. The violin climbs to some high, pleading trills before closing gently on a reminiscence of the opening phrase. It is a charming piece and, if only as a fairly substantial encore to the Violin Concerto, would well merit revival.

Another short concertante violin piece, the *Valse-scherzo* (Op. 34), was dedicated to Yosif Kotek, a composition student of Tchaikovsky's as well as a close friend and the agent of his introduction to Nadezhda von Meck. Modest Tchaikovsky describes him as 'good-looking, big-hearted, enthusiastic and a talented virtuoso'. Like the *Sérénade,* it is cast in simple ternary form – a lively waltz tune, a more impassioned middle section, a return to the first theme with engaging virtuoso decorative figures playing about it.

Violin Concerto in D

Auer, Kotek and Brodsky were all to feature in the production of the Violin Concerto in D (Op. 35) to which these works form a prelude. Staying in Clarens in 1878 while recovering from his disastrous marriage, Tchaikovsky was visited by Kotek and the two spent much time together playing over various unfamiliar pieces. With advice from Kotek on the solo violin writing, he worked on the new concerto with such enthusiasm that it was fully sketched within the month of March and scored by the end of April. On 1 April he played the first movement through with Kotek to Modest: they were both delighted, but their dissatisfaction with the *andante* led Tchaikovsky to discard it in favour of the present movement. The rejected piece he used as *Méditation* in the *Trois Morceaux* (Op. 42), published under the title *Souvenir d'un lieu cher*. It is a pleasant piece, but Kotek and Modest were right, as Tchaikovsky saw, in feeling it too slight and indeed sentimental for the slow movement of a major concerto. However, the new movement was insufficient to persuade Auer of the concerto's merits, despite its temporary dedication to him, and he proceeded to respond in the same manner as Rubinstein had over the First Piano Concerto, as Tchaikovsky related in his 1888 Diary:

> He pronounced it impossible to play, and this verdict, coming from such an authority as the Petersburg virtuoso, had the effect of casting this unfortunate child of my imagination for many years to come into the limbo of hopelessly forgotten things.

Kotek – to whom it had been dedicated before Auer – likewise abandoned his plan to learn the work; and for over two years it remained unperformed. Eventually Tchaikovsky heard from Jürgenson, who had meanwhile published the score, that Brodsky had learned the work and was planning to play it at a Vienna Philharmonic concert under Hans Richter. The first performance was on 4 December 1881, and caused an uproar in the hall, with demonstrations for Brodsky and against the work; and Hanslick, in a vituperative attack, was moved to suggest that the work actually gave off a bad smell. Tchaikovsky, who chanced upon this review in a Rome café, was deeply wounded and the more grateful to Brodsky, who kept up his championship of the work and well earned its rededication to him. Auer continued to pattern his behaviour on Rubinstein's, for he changed his opinion of the work and became one of its most notable exponents: further, as one of the greatest teachers of his day he was to introduce it to many of its most famous interpreters (Heifetz and Elman were among his pupils).

As with the First Piano Concerto, the opening melody (on first violins) proves to have no further role to play in the work; there is a similar sense of generalised introduction, of an instrument and its particular character being presented before the musical action

begins – here a gentle, lyrical personality, whose virtuoso elements
we do not yet glimpse. By the tenth bar, however, the violins have
introduced a rhythmic figure which builds up towards a climax and
proves, when the soloist has entered with a brief unaccompanied
passage that casts an oblique glance at the opening, to be the
substance of the first theme. The second subject is similar in
spirit: it is as if Tchaikovsky wished to present this lyrical side of
the violin as its most prominent characteristic, leaving its virtuoso
abilities for connecting passages and for the ornamentation of the
themes. Even in the cadenza, the virtuosity is turned towards the
enhancement of the two themes, not presented for the sake of fire-
works nor even as an inherent characteristic of the violin. This in
turn places the burden of carrying climaxes upon the orchestra
alone; and though the scoring is at times rather harsh, there is a
very ingenious dramatic balance between solo and orchestra, both
in the alternation of solo and *tutti* throughout the course of this
sonata movement, and in devising orchestral figuration which will
allow the violin to be heard in its most elaborately decorative
passages without being required to force its tone or seem to
dominate the orchestra.

As with the majority of classical violin concertos, the key is D
major (the open strings of the violin are G-D-A-E, which in D are
the subdominant, tonic, dominant, and dominant of the dominant,
the key-pattern around which events are likely to move). Tchaikovsky's original slow movement was in D minor, providing
insufficient key-contrast; the piece he substituted is in G minor,
the subdominant minor. This turning of the music towards a
flatter key further emphasises the tender side of the instrument;
and Tchaikovsky is at pains to show this emotional transition by
a brief passage, opening the movement, in which woodwind and
horns lead the music from D major into G minor. In this key the
soloist enters, over muted upper strings, with a melody that justi-
fies the movement's title 'Canzonetta'. There is a more fervent
answering theme before the return of the canzonetta, this time
decorated with characteristic woodwind figuration, and ending
now in D. The link with the finale is beautifully managed: from
D the opening woodwind passage leads on to a seventh chord for
strings, who proceed to exchange with the woodwind a simple
figure alternating one of the notes in the succeeding chord sequence

with the note beneath it. When the finale crashes suddenly in with an orchestral *tutti,* it is in the key of A which has been carefully anticipated, and on a vigorous version of the alternating-note figure which proves to be the substance of the main theme of the finale:

EX. 17

The side of the violin's character introduced with this theme (which consists of hardly more than the little figure quoted, together with a couple of bars of semiquaver figuration linking it to its next statement) has a distinct folk element; indeed this vigorous dance produces a second theme in which, over droning bagpipe fifths and a dour bassoon counterpoint, the violin has a melody based on Tchaikovsky's characteristically folkish falling fourths:

EX. 18

This works itself up into a wild dance, more delicately answered by woodwind before the return of the first theme. Out of these two elements the finale is composed; and as in the first movement the very considerable virtuosity which the writing demands is always directed towards decoration of the theme, towards heightening of the 'lyrical idea', rather than as a display of the violin's technical capabilities. The concerto remains among the most testing in the Romantic repertory; but the violinists who have succeeded best with it are those who have treated it as fundamentally a lyrical and not a virtuoso work.

Variations on a Rococo Theme

Tchaikovsky's homage to the spirit of his beloved Mozart is less effectively expressed in his *Mozartiana* suite than in the *Variations on a Rococo Theme* (Op. 33), which owe their origin to the composer's friendship with the German cellist Wilhelm Fitzenhagen but their impulse to his typically Romantic yearning for the grace and poise he felt to have passed out of music with the eighteenth century. The theme is his own, a carefully constructed melody that contrives to be at once classical in manner yet entirely personal in its cast of phrase:

EX. 19

The shape of the variations is equally classical. After a short orchestral introduction the cello plays the theme, which is answered by a woodwind ritornello with cello reply that can also serve as link between variations. These are seven in number. No. 1 decorates the theme in running triplets, and is joined by the ritornello and answer to No. 2. This concentrates on the opening notes in exchanges between cello and orchestra, set against light, rapid cello scales; the variation is in Tchaikovsky's most delicate 'ballet' vein. The key changes from the basic A major to C major for variation 3, a graceful *andante sostenuto* decorated on its return after a pause bar by softly chiming woodwind triplets. The ritornello figure is itself varied at the end of the variation, which turns back to A major for variation 4, combining theme and ritornello in an *andante grazioso*. Both these are passed to the orchestra alone for variation 5, with the cello concentrating, in a manner familiar from the concertos, on brilliant decorative passages between orchestral *tutti* and woodwind statements. The natural outcome for the cello is a cadenza, leading now towards D minor for variation 6, a comparatively straight treatment of the theme over plucked strings. Hitherto theme and ritornello have been subjected to the lightest variation; in variation 7 they are developed much more substantially in a brilliant *allegro vivo*. Not only these thematic elements but the gradual lightening and fragmentation of the orchestration are developed to a new extreme, the cello busying itself with the swiftest exchanges with the orchestra and the ritornello figure, which began as no more than a highly decorated cadential figure, now becoming fully thematic. Thus the variation sums the work up in a threefold manner – by a final development of the rococo theme, by producing the most brilliant orchestration based on the theme's component parts, and by bringing the ritornello figure into full relationship with the theme it had begun by merely attending. It is a satisfying conclusion to a work of immense charm and wit.

Pezzo Capriccioso, Op. 62

The *Pezzo capriccioso* (Op. 62) of 1887 was written for another of Tchaikovsky's cellist friends, Anatoly Brandukov, and is on the scale of the *Sérénade mélancolique*. Despite its title, it is a grave piece composed in the same key as the *Pathétique,* B minor. Although the cello takes part in the introduction, the main theme does not appear at first: it is a gentle melody based on a simple rising scale (and, typically, set against a descending scale accompaniment). The figuration grows more elaborate, although the basic pace and mood do not change even with a demisemiquaver passage in D major. This survives a return to the manner of the opening; and it is on a figure of energetically bowed demisemiquavers similar to the ending of the *Rococo Variations* that the piece closes. It is capricious in the sense of being a fancy, a brief toying with a mood in its various aspects, rather than as a *jeu d'esprit*; but it does not deserve its almost total neglect by cellists who take enthusiastically to the Variations, and in its modest way is both original and touching. Fitzenhagen as well as Brandukov contributed expert knowledge to the solo writing; and on 7 December 1889 Tchaikovsky conducted Brandukov in the first performance at a concert which included Beethoven's Ninth Symphony.

MANFRED

Outside the set of Tchaikovsky's six symphonies, yet separate from the suites and symphonic poems, lies *Manfred*. It was a work about which he always felt ambivalent: to Emilia Pavlovskaya, the singer and friend who proposed *Eugene Onegin* to him as a subject, he declared that, for all the work involved in it, it was perhaps the best of his symphonic compositions, and he repeated the opinion to his publisher Jürgenson; but to the Grand Duke Constantine he asserted that it was abominable, and Taneyev was told:

> It's a thousand times more pleasing to write without a programme. Composing a programme-symphony, I have the sensation of being a charlatan and cheating the public; I am paying them not hard cash but rubbishy bits of paper money.

However, as he also told Taneyev, he felt under an obligation to Balakirev, who had for some time been pestering him to write the work and had even supplied him with detailed synopses, key-patterns and suggestions for orchestration.

The first idea for *Manfred* goes back to Berlioz's second and final visit to Russia in the winter of 1867–8. Among the works he conducted was *Harold in Italy*; and to the leaders of Russian music, eagerly congregated at his concerts, the work came as a revelation. Here was not only a major symphonic work outside the German tradition, but a successful handling of the theme of the Romantic outsider by one of the most brilliant musicians of the day; moreover, the European enthusiasm for Byron had come, typically, late to Russia and was still running high. The immediate outcome was Rimsky-Korsakov's *Antar*, another symphony with a programme and a motto theme to identify the hero. At the same time, the critic Stasov proposed to Balakirev the scheme for a symphony on the next most obvious Byron subject of the Romantic outsider, *Manfred*. That the poem is far from Byron's most distinguished mattered little: it was doubtless the portrait of Manfred as a guilty, doomed sensibility that made an effective appeal to one aspect of the Russian temperament. Stasov's programme proposed a work in four movements. In the first, Manfred wanders in the Alps, shattered and remorseful, troubled by the past and seeking oblivion; from time to time there steal into his mind memories of his ideal love, Astarte. The second movement depicts the simple life of the Alpine hunters, its ease and delight presenting a rueful contrast to Manfred's gloom. In the third movement, the Alpine fairy, appearing in a waterfall, gives the opportunity of a scherzo. The finale suggests a wild *Allegro*, an orgy in the underground palace of Arimanes; Astarte appears once more before pandemonium resumes and the works ends (*Largo*) with Manfred's death.

Balakirev was not convinced that this proposal suited his own talents; but never happier than when running his colleagues' creative lives for them, he set about placing the idea. The obvious first candidate was Berlioz himself; and in 1868, attempting to reinforce his arguments with a comparison of Byron's rejection by England to Berlioz's own rejection by France, he sent Stasov's scenario to Berlioz, passing it off as his own. But Berlioz, exhausted and within months of death, showed no interest; and there the matter rested for some fourteen years. Then, in 1882, Balakirev had occasion to write to Tchaikovsky with a belated acknowledgement of the dedication of *Romeo and Juliet*; and no doubt feeling that he had acted very successfully as godfather to that work by outlining its programme, he now tried to tempt Tchaikovsky with the idea for a symphonic poem. Interested, Tchaikovsky asked if he could be sent details; and once again Balakirev sent off the Stasov scenario, together with a number of characteristic admonitions: there is to be an *idée fixe*, depicting Manfred himself, appearing in all four movements, the key-scheme is closely detailed, the nature of the Astarte music is described, and there is a stern warning about the necessity of avoiding banality in the pastoral movement:

Of course at the beginning you'll have to have something suggesting hunting, but in doing so you must be *particularly careful not to fall into the banal*. God preserve you from vulgarities in the manner of German fanfares and *Jägermusik*.

He concludes, after some more instructions about how to write the flute, parts on the same stave, with the comment,

As you see, I want your future masterpiece to be ideal in every detail, with nothing perfunctory. This subject is not only profound but contemporary, for the sickness of modern man lies in the fact that he cannot preserve his ideals. They are shattered, nothing is left for the satisfaction of the soul except bitterness. Hence all the troubles of our time.

Tchaikovsky was far from convinced by this. In a long letter of 24 November 1882 from his sister's house at Kamenka, he protests first that he has no translation of *Manfred* (he did by this stage of his life read English quite well, but would obviously have preferred a Russian version: there is a four-volume French translation of Byron on his bookshelves at Klin). He next disclaims Balakirev's suggestion that *Francesca da Rimini* and *The Tempest* represent his 'apogee', and goes on to point out, very reasonably, that what would clearly suit Berlioz well was not necessarily sound material for his own music:

I agree that, following it, there could be constructed an effective symphony in the style of that composer. But it leaves me at present completely cold, and when heart and imagination are unwarmed, it is hardly worth trying to compose.

Later he adds,

I do not at all think that programme music *à la* Berlioz is in general a false form of art, but merely mention the fact that I have done nothing remarkable in this sphere.

He concludes that his admiration for Schumann's *Manfred* has entirely associated the text with different music (history does not relate whether Balakirev noticed that this gives the lie to Tchaikovsky's initial evasions that he must wait until he had read the poem). There matters rested for two years, until Balakirev and Tchaikovsky met in St Petersburg in 1884 at the first performance in the Imperial Theatres of *Eugene Onegin*. They discussed *Manfred* again, and Balakirev gave him a new version of the scenario together with a list of recommended works which, apart from anything else, reflects the contemporary anxiety among Russians to construct their own music on the best European models: the works include Liszt's *Hamlet*, the finale of *Harold in Italy* and three Chopin preludes for the first and last movements, the *Scène aux Champs* for the *Adagio*, and the Queen Mab scherzo from Berlioz's *Romeo and Juliet* for the scherzo; two of Tchaikovsky's own works are also urged upon him. By November, Tchaikovsky was writing back to say that he at last intended to write the work. Sketches were begun in April 1885. By 25 September he was able to write to Balakirev with the news that, though he had been obliged to depart in places from his instructions, the symphony was now complete. The apology alone indicates how much he, like others of his generation, was under the spell of this dynamic, intelligent musician; and it is reinforced by the fact that in his eagerness to show Balakirev how well he had done, he anticipates the actual conclusion of the work, for another letter to his brother Modest a week later reports that he has not in fact finished. The scoring was not completed until 4 October.

Tchaikovsky's hesitations and vacillations about the work, both before and after he composed it, are not hard to understand. He knew he was composing something that probably lay against his true artistic nature, yet the subject had its attractions for him – there was particularly the fascination with Manfred as a guilt-wracked, lonely sensibility doomed to frustration in love – and Balakirev, a very articulate and convincing colleague, had been proved right in the past over his first masterpiece, *Romeo and Juliet*. In the Fourth Symphony, composed almost eight years previously, he had discovered for the first time a way of reconciling an emotional programme to the demands of symphonic form: it must have seemed improbable that this approach to the symphony as a form could yield further gains, and the notion of a symphonic work that took its form from a character study in the imagination rather than from autobiography must have seemed attractive. There was his natural dislike of programme music to overcome; yet the subject and its eventual treatment are in fact no more programmatic than the details of the Fourth Symphony revealed to Nadezhda von Meck.

Though Berlioz inevitably remains the father-figure to the symphony, Tchaikovsky has well understood how the subject might be made his own. He resists the use of a solo instrument: the essence of the viola soloist in *Harold in Italy* is that the hero remains outside all the vivid action, his nature declared in the first movement but his person thereafter able to observe, even participate in, but never truly be united with, the pilgrims and Abruzzi mountaineers and even the Romantically liberated brigands with their unconfined orgy. For Tchaikovsky, the hero must move in and out of the events described, his recurring theme being sufficient to mark the points at which he stands back in isolation and is, by new treatment in harmony or orchestration, newly portrayed as he moves through the plot. Tchaikovsky could readily accept the merit of Berlioz's design whereby a long,

reflective first movement declaring the nature of the hero is succeeded by two lighter interlude movements and rounded off by
a Bacchanal (replacing the Orgy); for this is a plan whose general
outlines he had himself already evolved as a method of symphonic thinking, and he would have had no difficulty in accepting
Balakirev's suggestion that the appropriate ending (and a more
musically and dramatically satisfying one than in *Harold*) would
be with Manfred's death. Moreover, freed from the necessity of
making some reconciliation with sonata form for his first movement, he devises a form of his own that is remarkably successful
in providing a satisfying structure and a firm base for the remainder
of the work. The movement is prefaced, in the final of Balakirev's
many versions as Tchaikovsky accepted it:

Manfred wanders in the Alps. Weary of the fatal questions of existence,
tormented by hopeless longings and the memory of past crimes, he suffers
cruel spiritual pangs. He has plunged into the occult sciences and commands
the mighty powers of darkness, but neither they nor anything in *this* world
can give him the *forgetfulness* to which alone he vainly aspires. The memory of
the lost Astarte, once passionately loved by him, gnaws at his heart and there
is neither limit nor end to Manfred's despair.

Manfred's theme is declared at the outset, a gloomy falling
melody accompanied by a characteristic figure on a descending
scale and starkly harmonised:

EX. 20

This has as its immediate answer a figure which remains
associated with Manfred:

EX. 21

The marking is *Lento lugubre*: as so often in Tchaikovsky, the section serves as a slow introduction, but the pace of the movement proper is no faster than *andante*, a section in which Ex. 21 is to some extent developed before the appearance of the vision of Astarte:

EX. 22

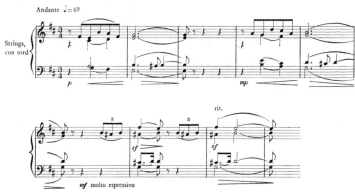

This has the dramatic effect of a second subject; but though the theme does reappear, there is no formal role as a second subject which it has to play, for the remainder of the movement concerns itself with Manfred himself, his vision lost and his aspect despairing.

After this powerful movement, firmly constructed and subjective in nature, effective symphonic contrast is provided by the two central genre pieces. Not only does their lightness of manner provide relief from the heaviness of the first movement, with its dark harmony and sombre orchestration: there is the true Romantic irony in the depiction of the elegant apparition of the Alpine fairy (Byron's Witch of the Alps) and of the cheerful, uncaring mountain people as set beside Manfred's vast despair. Though

Tchaikovsky probably had not read Rousseau, his familiarity with Tolstoy's *The Cossacks* and his interpretation of it in his Fourth Symphony were sufficient to give him a feeling for this essential Romantic notion. The second movement is marked *Vivace con spirito* and headed 'The Alpine Fairy appears before Manfred in the rainbow of a waterfall'. The image of the colours suspended in the dancing spray gives Tchaikovsky the opportunity for some of his most enchanting orchestration, scored with a brilliance and lightness that Berlioz himself would have admired as strings and woodwind sparkle and patter in delicate figuration: it is one of his longest and most skilfully worked scherzos. When the Alpine Fairy herself is revealed in the Trio, her features prove to bear an unmistakably Slavonic cast:

EX. 23

The third movement, Pastorale, depicts 'The simple, free and peaceful life of the mountain people'. Balakirev had evidently hoped for a Russian version of the *Scène aux champs*, but Tchaikovsky provides something which takes its nature from the third movement of *Harold in Italy*: Manfred's appearance, as in the previous movement, is as a briefly glimpsed observer, and there is neither the mysterious shadow that comes over the music in the closing pages of Berlioz's *Scène aux champs* nor the intervention of Harold among the Abruzzi mountaineers. There is, nevertheless, something of Berlioz in the gentle, touchingly harmonised oboe melody of the opening:

EX. 24.

The finale is headed 'The underground palace of Arimanes. Manfred appears in the middle of the Bacchanale. Evocation of the shade of Astarte. She foretells the end of his earthly sufferings. Death of Manfred.' The movement again recalls *Harold* in the somewhat factitious exuberance of the revels; but Tchaikovsky tries to balance the effective episodic structure of the opening movement by means of an excellent fugue (one of the best in all his work), a dramatically well-placed return of Astarte, and (with the organ or harmonium which was among Balakirev's specifications) a finely conceived death scene.

Manfred was first performed in Moscow on 11 March 1886, with Max Erdmannsdörfer conducting. Tchaikovsky himself, uncertain as he was of whether the work was his best or 'an abomination', refused to accept payment from Jürgenson or from his Paris publisher Félix Mackar for a work he believed would seldom be performed; and in the moments in which he despised everything except the first movement he made plans to rewrite it as a symphonic poem. He never did; and for this we may be grateful. The faults of *Manfred*, the most basic of which derives from Tchaikovsky's difficulty in handling thematic transformation with the inventive assurance of Liszt, are greatly outweighed by its merits. The programme symphonies of the nineteenth century were by their nature dealing with empirical forms, and it is easy to point to works in which enthusiasm for the subject has distorted a composer's appreciation of musical balance. Wary as he was of the subject and doubtful of his own ability to master it, Tchaikovsky took exceptional care with the form of the work. Though this does not relate closely to classical principles even as they are made amenable to Tchaikovsky's thought in his six numbered symphonies, it has a symmetry and within this a variety which release some of his most powerful and most charming music. His greatest music was to be produced by the contact between his own personal situation and the demands of a basically classical symphonic form;

and it was the awareness in *Manfred* of the need to contrive solutions that perhaps aroused unnecessary doubts in the mind of a composer for whom the 'lyrical idea' was the purest music and anything that betrayed contrivance was held to be unworthy. But in its success in reconciling different expressive demands, in discovering a form that would be true to the subject and would frame characteristic and well-composed music, *Manfred* can rank as one of the great programme symphonies of the nineteenth century.

'Music is not illusion, but revelation rather,' Tchaikovsky wrote to Nadezhda von Meck in 1877. 'Its triumphant power resides in the fact that it reveals to us beauties we find nowhere else, and that the apprehension of them is not transitory, but a perpetual reconcilement to life.' When he did indulge his need to escape into an artificial, consciously pretty world, he conquered it with some of the finest ballet music ever composed, scores that set a standard and formed a style which was still to be influencing composers as different as Prokofiev and Britten over half a century later. The histrionic side of his character, one whose exaggerations and even insincerities he recognised and bewailed, found one form of expression in his concertos, whether by way of the artistic device of the 'rococo' theme for one of his most charming works or in the full panoply of a piano concerto that presents a character as dramatic, as lyrical and as demonstrative as himself. But this was not his true inner self, and not even the concertos lie close to the centre of his character. A man who acknowledges his own insincerity is not fundamentally insincere; and though Tchaikovsky's self-pity, self-love and self-hatred lie far from the tragic strength of his admired Beethoven, we must beware of denying it a heroic quality because we find it lacking in toughness or noble reticence. Like many homosexuals, Tchaikovsky was fascinated above all by his own sensations; but he never willingly fell from the high standards he set himself as an artist. A lesser composer, given his temperament and talent, could have squandered it on trivia. Tchaikovsky's self-awareness extended to a shrewd assessment of his gift and its potentialities. The composer of the first three symphonies – works that are still underrated – could have made a highly successful career in the concert hall and left a legacy of half a dozen more such delightful works. Yet he sensed that symphonic form, for which he was by nature ill-equipped, posed a challenge and offered a high opportunity. When he emphasised his formal deficiencies, he was putting his finger on a palpable defect; like some of his critics, he seems to have underestimated the creative triumph involved in bringing even his touch with ballet music into a symphonic experience – not as diversion or contrast, a modern extension of the minuet and trio, but for proper expressive purposes, as the structure of a complex emotional situation.

This, surely, is what he had in mind when he asked that music should be not illusion but revelation; and if he failed to win true reconcilement to life, the music that records the struggle is that of an artist who, however much he may have felt bound to present an artificial front to the world, tried to face the bitter truth to himself.

INDEX